KRIS WHITEHEAD

BECOMING ICONIC

HOW TO MAKE
TODAY'S CEILING
TOMORROW'S FLOOR

Edited by Hilary Jastram and Dave Rynne

Dedication

First, this book is dedicated to my beautiful wife, Robyn. You are a warrior in your own right, and I am blessed beyond measure for having you as a best friend in life. You, quite literally, have made me a better human.

I also want to thank my late friend, mentor, and business partner, Lonnie Robinson. Your untimely passing is a reminder to me that tomorrow is NEVER guaranteed and that even beyond the grave, I am still learning from you, brother. Thank you for being a living example of what it means to help others succeed. Thank you for standing in the gap and helping me realize WHO I am, WHAT I want, and ALWAYS seeing the best in me. Godspeed, brother, may we meet again.

Finally, I want to dedicate this book to EVERY entrepreneur who is in the thick of it. It ain't all sunshine and rainbows, is it? There are so many tests along this path, most of which will remain with you, unheralded, unheard, and unspoken.

You have chosen YOU. You are in a brotherhood/sisterhood of the highest order because you decided to take a chance on yourself. Like all of us who have, I know you "get it." It's the willingness to throw away mediocrity and truly see what you're capable of achieving.

There is NO retiring from YOU. It's a rare person in this world who's willing to ignore the certainty of getting paid regularly for the opportunity to find out what you're really worth.

I salute you, and I hope this book will inspire you to continue to evolve into who you are truly meant to be. Whether we ever meet or not, you are family. Thank you for striving to make a difference in the world by showing everyone how unique and valuable you truly are.

Resources

Facebook

Group: Facebook.com/groups/ThinkToSucceedMastermind

Personal: Facebook.com/TheKrisWhitehead

LinkedIn

LinkedIn.com/in/KrisWhitehead/

Instagram

Instagram.com/Kris_Whitehead_Official/

Website

www.KrisWhitehead.com

"It is not the critic who counts; not the man who points out how the strong man stumbles or where the doer of deeds could have done them better.

The credit belongs to the man who is actually in the arena, whose face is marred by dust and sweat and blood;

Who strives valiantly; who errs, who comes short again and again, because there is no effort without error and shortcoming;

But who does actually strive to do the deeds; who knows great enthusiasms, the great devotions; who spends himself in a worthy cause;

Who at the best knows, in the end, the triumph of high achievement, and who at the worst, if he fails, at least fails while daring greatly, so that his place shall never be with those cold and timid souls who neither know victory nor defeat."

—Theodore Roosevelt

In the trenches...

One of the ideas of being someone of worth is the ability to still be standing when the smoke of battle clears.

For your significant other, clients, employees ... anyone to be able to trust you, they need the ability to believe that you have what it takes to stay the course.

If you're doing it right, entrepreneurship is a lonely road, and if you're doing it wrong ... it's even lonelier.

Most people will never understand why you're willing to sacrifice so much.

Most people will never understand why you're willing to invest the time, endure the stress, and delay gratification. So much so that, at times, you might feel like the rest of the world has "it" figured out, as you chose to chase a pipedream that just won't work.

Trust me ... I know.

With more than two decades of leading others, I've had to learn many of the lessons I'm going to share in these pages the hard way. I've been forced to face my limiting beliefs and put my anger, fears, and frustrations aside only to find that ALL OF THOSE FEELINGS were still there, bearing "interest."

I came to the conclusion that I needed to upgrade the quality of information I consumed and those I chose to allow to influence my thinking.

Sometimes, the pressure of impending failure and the feeling of desperation from few to no options left had me finally bending a knee, bowing my head, and giving it all to my Higher Power.

This is where I began to understand that I wasn't alone.

This is also where I began to understand that I had a choice to make.

Most likely, the MOST important choice to make, too.

Was I doing business to make money, or was I choosing a lifestyle that gave me immediate feedback on whether I was creating a life worth living?

Owning a business is living in the "hot seat." As you grow, I promise that it doesn't get easier; you simply get better. And your business is a jealous mistress. If you quit paying attention to it, give it any indication you aren't in it for the long haul, or abuse it ... retribution will follow.

So, when my "enthusiasm" for quick riches faded over the years, I had a choice to make. One you'll have to make too if you aim to have sustainable success over the long haul.

Are you dabbling at entrepreneurship, or are you going to BURN THE SHIP and face your enemy HEAD ON with no means of retreat?

That, my friend, is when you, too, are in the trenches.

That trench is meant for all of us who need the respite, the shelter, and the strategies to win the war of business.

The trenches are where you'll find ICONIC men and women who live, breathe, and bleed for their cause.

The trenches are where you learn that what you perceived as the best you can do simply isn't. You will learn to dream bigger because you have no choice if you want to survive the battles of business. In so doing, you will see that your perceived ceiling is only limited to what you are certain you can achieve.

The trenches will reveal to you that you are capable of so much more, and you will learn that today's limits are only obstacles to overcome. You will learn to trust your intuition and live in a flow-state of certainty.

The reason you are only finding out this information now is that you haven't been ready. But operating without certainty will get you killed on real battlefields, as well as the metaphorical ones in business—so this is a necessary mindset shift.

Come on and hop in the trench with me, give me your best war cry, point that gun down range ... and let's get to doing some damage on the enemy.

I promise, it's going to be the fight of your life, and one day, a long time from now, when you look back at the choice you made to get in the trenches with me, I hope you realize that it was your CERTAINTY that led to you VICTORY.

Let's go...

Down into the trenches...

Table of Contents

Foreword 1

Introduction 5

Chapter 1: On Becoming Iconic 9

Chapter 2: Living for the Moment 23

Chapter 3: Maximum Effort Will Fail You Every Single
Time 29

Chapter 4: Focus on Solutions 35

Chapter 5: Does Your Tenacity Match Your Capacity? 41

Chapter 6: What Kind of Man Are You? 45

Chapter 7: Mastering the Monotony 51

Chapter 8: Your Vision, Your Values, and Your Verdict 59

Chapter 9: Slaying Your Superman Syndrome 67

Chapter 10: Relationships Are the New Reward 71

Chapter 11: What Master Do You Really Serve? 77

Chapter 12: You Weren't Born to Ask Permission 81

Chapter 13: You Can Be Right, or You Can Win 87

Chapter 14: Busier than Hell and Still Not Winning? 91

Chapter 15: Climbing the Summit of Success 99

Chapter 16: If Not Now…When? 107

Chapter 17: There is No Plan B 111

Chapter 18: How Are You Showing Up? 115

Chapter 19: Running the Red Line..119

Chapter 20: Becoming the Champion of Change 123

Chapter 21: The Real Function of Fear 127

Chapter 22: "No" is a Complete Sentence 131

Chapter 23: Just Because You Bought It, Doesn't Mean
    You Own It..135

Chapter 24: Who Will Do What by When? 139

Chapter 25: Power Versus Force...145

Afterword 153

About the Author 155

Disclaimer 157

Foreword

I met Kris Whitehead, as I've met many high-level entrepreneurs when he came into Apex Executives and was assigned to me as a coaching client. I will never forget our first call. I was in Indianapolis, Indiana, at a trade show called *The Work Truck Show*, and our first call was scheduled in between some of my meetings there. I remember sneaking out to one of the hallways in the convention center to have that call, which was only supposed to be 30 minutes, and it ended up lasting an hour. Normally, I would have been frustrated by that, but my initial reaction to Kris was powerful.

Kris had come to Apex through his brother, Jonathan Lautermilch, who was already a member. Kris told me on that call that he didn't know what Apex was all about but that he was interested in seeing where being a member would go. During that first conversation, we realized we had a lot of similarities in our stories. He had faced a lot of the same struggles in his first business that I had in mine. And his experience of having that business crash and burn mirrored mine in such a way as to create a deep understanding between us. The guy flat out told me on our first call, "I don't know why I'm saying this, but you are I are going to be close friends." Now, total honesty here; I kind of wrote it off when he said that. I thought to myself, *okay, whatever. This is just somebody else coming into the network for me to coach.* But what he said that day was the truth. We did become close friends.

I started getting on coaching calls with Kris and learning more about him and his business. Now, Kris was one of those clients who didn't need to be coached all the time. However, when Kris needed me, he had no problem reaching out. And Kris reached out to me a couple of times and said, "This is what I'm struggling with. This is what I see ..." He's a very observant man. Kris looks at things from all different angles, and he's very deep. Because of this, he and I had deep and in-depth conversations about life, purpose, spirituality, and everything in between.

One of the events we put on for our Apex Executives is a monthly in-person session called Fly in Fridays (FIF). This is when our most elite clients come to the office, and the entire team spends a full day coaching them face to face. Kris didn't go to them all the time, but I'll never forget his first FIF. After the event was over, we walked around the corner to a restaurant to have dinner. Kris sat at the head of the table, and I sat right next to him. He started asking about the book writing and publishing process, so I laid it all out for him. I told him where he would most likely get stuck, how to get around that, and what the entire process from start to finish would look like. Kris walked away from that conversation with his head spinning, but here we are a year and a half later, and he's written his book.

On top of that, Kris has been building and scaling his construction business. He built out the SOPs (Standard Operating Procedures) for his business and has created such a well-oiled machine that he hardly ever has to work IN the business. Now, don't get me wrong, the man works and works hard. But he has built out his processes and businesses to the point that now he can take on other projects and focus on them because his business is basically running itself. He literally unfucked his business the way I tell people to do in my book, *Unf*ck Your Business.* He built a business that can operate without him being there every day.

It's pretty wild to see the evolution Kris has gone through over these last two years. After COVID hit, and he had to fight — just like everyone else — to keep his business afloat, he went to work. Honestly, there's no other way to put it. He became laser-focused on becoming the most elite version of himself. He started diving in and doing everything we ask our people to do when they come into the Apex Executives network. He started interacting. He started showing up, both for himself and for the rest of the people in the program. It didn't take long before Kris proved himself to be a true leader.

He took initiative and hosted live pop-up events. When he would come down here to Dallas, I would see him corral people like me, his brother, Jonathan Lautermilch, Marc Zalmanoff, and a couple of other people. He'd say, "I'm going to gather 15, 20, 30 people. We're just going to host a little event here in the lobby of the Break Free Academy office if that's cool with you guys. We're going to help people and influence them." Sure enough, Kris started putting together mini-events and changing people's lives. You see, when Kris talks, people listen. He speaks with passion. He's genuine. He's intelligent, and he's got real-world experience that applies to many different people on many different levels. Whether he's talking about business, relationships, parenting, or life in general, he gives it to you straight and from the heart.

That, my friend, is why I believe this book matters so much. Kris' book is going to help people immensely. Not just business owners, either, but people who are struggling in any area of life. Kris takes his lived experiences and extracts the lessons from them. He frames them in such a way that they're relatable to just about anyone willing to listen. Kris isn't some guy simply coming up with ideas and spouting off, he has been in the trenches, and he knows what it takes to get to the top. He also knows what it means to burn it all down and start over.

So, you have two choices here … You can continue to smash your head against the wall, or you can get deeply involved and take what is written here in this book to heart and apply it to your life. I promise you, if you do the latter, you will be well on your way to becoming the most elite version of yourself and building both the life and business of your dreams.

Tomas Keenan

COO, Break Free Academy, Founder, Step It Up Enterprises

Bestselling Author, *Unf*ck Your Business*

Introduction

There's your truth, someone else's truth, and the actual truth. It takes the ability to see all sides to find the path that leads to harmony.

Just like finding any point in the universe, you need three distinct points to triangulate it.

This book is about being an agent of change.

I've been an agent of change my entire life. From my parents divorcing when I was two years old and never getting along to being an all-star baseball player and the lead in plays on stage, I've always been told I had to choose a single parent, a certain set of friends, and a singular path.

Why?

Why do I have to choose between Mom OR Dad?

Why do I have to choose one career?

Why do I have to choose to be part of a particular social class?

Can't I be friends with the jocks, metalheads, rednecks, the homophobic, the homosexual, etc.?

My problem was that I never knew where I fit in.

For the most part, I found a way to "get in" everywhere; I just wasn't allowed to stay. The moment I had contrary ideas to any particular group, I found myself "politely" ushered to the outside.

If you've ever felt the same way, this book is for you.

It's a book about searching for foundational truths that will always be a bedrock—and knowing that with these, you can build anything you want in life.

Each chapter is designed to help you first recognize a common stumbling block in life and/or business. Then, the goal is to help you see opportunities and techniques for creating a new pathway to overcome the challenge. Finally, just because you understand something doesn't mean you'll do the work required to see the result. With that in mind, each chapter also includes what I've done and taught others to do to find the success we all seek.

These ideas will make you think, challenge your preconceived notions, and spur you toward clarity for YOUR intended goals.

Some people say that experience is the best teacher. My journey has taught me that other people's experiences can help me get what I want quicker without the pain from the lessons that would have ensued.

It's also been said that "the truth will set you free."

No, friend, the truth is only the truth. It's KNOWLEDGE of the truth that can shine a light on the path of your success.

Your PROPER application of knowledge will, in due course, give you the freedom you seek.

If you're looking for a step-by-step formula for success, this isn't it. For a long time, I wished for that very thing. But being an agent of change doesn't allow for a mechanical application of knowledge, and neither does being a free-thinking human.

There's always another mountain to climb, another question to ask, and more wisdom to be had. That's exactly what this book is designed to help you with. Like I said, there are three parts to each chapter. You can read the chapters in any order or simply pick a thought-provoking page.

When each chapter is read in total, it will drive the point home like this:

1. There is TRUTH (three types)
2. There is KNOWLEDGE of the truth
3. There is APPLICATION of knowledge, called WISDOM.

This is the BE, DO, HAVE way of accomplishing your goals.

Three simple steps to achieve anything you want in life.

But, if it's so simple, why do so few actually accomplish what they set out to do?

Worse, why do so many people get caught in the trap of settling for less than being who they're meant to be?

Among the top regrets of people who are at the end of their lives are caring too much about what others think, working too much, and not taking enough risks.

Why? Well, let's start at the beginning of how we all become indoctrinated into fitting into society. We're force-fed questions with only one right answer. At first, this is meant to give us "bumpers" to keep us on the pathway to survival.

Over time, it becomes a noose around most of our necks, keeping us from veering into truly exploring how very unique we are. Most people will settle for this noose.

You can recognize it's there in many ways. People who are in bondage will talk about life happening to them. They will reminisce on the accolades of past wins to the series of opportunities that were snatched from them just as they were about to win. They will use sarcastic undertones in almost every conversation and blame the mistrust of humanity on the dreams they won't work to achieve. Everything is ALWAYS someone else's fault in their minds...

And they're right.

I know because, for years, I fell for the bullshit conversations in my head that kept me playing in the safe zone.

This book is your opportunity to ask yourself if you're ready to play outside those norms. Are you ready to live a life of significance and give yourself the opportunity to find out how powerful you are?

No excuses are allowed when you play life without a safety net...

The idea of freedom and living life on our terms is the very definition of being true to ourselves. I want you to know that you aren't alone. You aren't the only "crazy" person out there who won't accept a "cookie-cutter life." One where you live the Monday through Friday life of a slave only to be a weekend warrior dreading the drive to work on Monday to provide for a family that you can't afford to invest any real time in.

Now that you've opened this book, you can ready yourself to live a life that broadcasts: "My life has real meaning, and I have no regrets."

Are you prepared to ask yourself pivotal questions to determine if you're *willing* to do the work?

I hope so because that's what we're going to explore.

That journey begins with a single step. Here's hoping you NEVER stop stepping!

Let's go...

Chapter 1

On Becoming Iconic

Never permit a dichotomy to rule your life, a dichotomy in which you hate what you do so you can have pleasure in your spare time. Look for a situation in which your work will give you as much happiness as your spare time.
—Pablo Picasso

Your First Exposure to Dichotomy

The definition of dichotomy, as described in Merriam-Webster, is "A division or contrast between two things that are or are represented as being opposed or entirely different."

I want to start here because this book will help you if you can fathom that you don't know everything and learn to ask the RIGHT questions.

Let's begin:

When we're young, our authorities give us the questions. You have to find the right answers. This is our first exposure to living in a dichotomy.

When we're older, answers are everywhere, but we have to learn how to come up with the right questions.

In school, we're taught theory because it paints a picture of what reality is. We must learn practical application, but we are "corrected" when our answers don't match the authority's expectations. This is the beginning of losing OUR TRUTH. Most of us aren't strong enough to withstand the barrage of criticism that keeps us inside the "circle of trust," or better said, inside the noose.

> **Over time, we learn that living a life of purpose
> and discipline leads to freedom of choice and
> more opportunities to create those choices.**

If you evade painful experiences, you end up having a hard life. What seems easy, avoiding tough or painful choices, is actually keeping you inside of mediocrity. If you do what's hard, meaning you work at finding YOUR answers by asking the RIGHT questions, and push yourself by following your instincts, life becomes easier.

As you read this book, I want you to remember we are each the hero in our own story.

By sharing my story with you, I hope to inspire you to embrace your own journey, no matter its challenges, tragedies, and triumphs. You can use these parts of your life to discover a renewed passion and an unwavering faith that you matter and that your story is not over.

I also want you to think about the fact that your joy is found in the journey, not in the destination.

I have shared my story with you in this book in the form of KEY LESSONS that I had to learn to move the needle forward and realize my dreams. MOST of these lessons are not categorized as "step-by-step," "do it and prove it." Rather, they are harder to see and harder to do; they involve intangible obstacles that I had to overcome to see the next step in my path.

My hope is that you can put yourself in my place as I share my experiences.

As I stated earlier, everyone is a hero in their own story.

But events, roadblocks, and logjams are going to happen when you live and work as an entrepreneur, and especially when you go for greatness.

I know that the right mindset and living a life of gratitude and purpose is the only way that you will want to pick yourself up, dust yourself off, and stay the course — until you receive rewards for the goals you've set for yourself.

What Do You Really Want?

It is understandable with all the confusion and well-meaning people around us that we would have no idea what we want out of life. Our focus is pulled all over the place.

My hope is to answer that question for you in this book: "What do you really want?"

This is a single question that leads to a single answer no matter where you are now, what obstacles you're facing, or the goals you have yet to achieve.

If you don't know what you want, that's perfectly natural. Many people don't. I also suspect that's why you cracked open this book!

Who Am I?

There are many factors to me, as there are to you.

Let's start with what I do. I currently own two companies and am an intrapreneur inside another:

- New England Custom Remodeling is a high-end, multi-million-dollar design/build company specializing in building additions, and kitchens, and bathrooms, serving the New England area.

- Iconic Mastermind Group services high-achieving elite-level entrepreneurs who wish to wring the absolute most out of life while they're here on Earth. My clients work with me one-on-one.

- I am the director for Apex Executive Coaches, an organization that helps financially successful business owners live their most elite lives.

Personally…

- I'm married to Robyn and am the proud father of three beautiful children.

- I love my family.

- I love my friends.

- I love my country.

Quite honestly, I love almost everyone I come across. Since my parents were divorced before I ever remember them being together, I've always tried to bring the "North" and "South" together. Look, I didn't create their hardships, so why am I responsible for someone CHOOSING to kick sand in someone's eyes instead of playing in the sandbox together, right?

Internally, it ate me alive. It was even harder when I was really young because it was normal to me. Dad would come visit and then leave. As I grew and saw other families together, I didn't blink an eye. My maternal grandfather was my dad in many regards, and whenever I was with my dad, we were in nature, taking baths in the river, walking on our properties while he marked trees for surveying (and I caught poison ivy all the damn time) or riding around on his motorcycle visiting his friends.

Where his absence really hit me was when school started. Somehow, not having Dad's presence daily created a desire to want everyone to accept me.

Let me better illustrate what I mean by sharing how confusing it all was back then:

I'd just moved back to my hometown in Southern Virginia from Baltimore. My stepdad had a stint up there in banking, but Mom was fed up with suburbia. It was the first day of sixth grade, and I was coming back after two years away.

I was nervous, but somehow, I knew that all eyes would be on me, and if I ever had a chance to get the attention I wanted, this … was … it.

The teacher introduced me to the class, and Rachel, oh how she'd blossomed. Michelle was looking at me, too … *gulp!*

Did she just flick her hair over her shoulder? Yeah, this is gonna be cool.

Greetings aside, I took my place in the rows of chairs, ready to chat at the first opportunity, but we got right into our subjects. My faded jean jacket sitting on the back of my chair and my L.L. Bean backpack let everyone know that I was a force to be reckoned with.

When the bell rang to end class, I was mobbed. The two Davids, Frank, Chris, Kathy, Joey, Rachel, Michelle, and about ten other kids, swarmed me. They asked probing questions, and I answered them like I was loftier and better than they were.

I mean, c'mon … this is hickville, and I've lived in the Baltimore metropolis.

That all worked out great until the lunch bell rang.

We ate lunch, and David asked, "What does your dad do?"

"He lives in Washington DC and travels around the world for business."

"Right, Whitehead."

"No, really, David. He does."

I don't remember the rest of lunch, but I do remember what happened next.

I followed Chris into the bathroom to pee. When we walked in, I saw five urinals lined up, side by side. Chris unbuttoned his pants and started peeing at the urinal, then walked backward while he was peeing.

I'm not kidding, he literally made it to the wall of sinks about ten feet from the urinal, and he was STILL hitting the hole in the porcelain … it was almost magical.

I'll never forget him squealing in a loud voice as he was hittin' the urinal, "Weeeeeeeeeeeee … weeeeeeeeeeeeeeeeeeee."

When he was done, he buttoned up, laughed at himself, and walked out.

I quietly saddled up to the urinal beside his and began to do my business. As I was finishing, Roosevelt, who was 6'4" and, I swear, 25 years old, but still in the sixth grade, came running in and tagged me.

He turned around and ran out. I took three large steps to chase him, and … whoops, on my face, I went.

Cold, hard, blue tiles … my skin touching … wet, cold tiles. That's all I remember.

As I walked back to class, I looked down at my soaked "What's the Beef?" yellow t-shirt. Then I started to cry, and dammit, it was ramping up with every step back to class.

As I walked in, crying and wet, I looked at the teacher and bellowed, "I slipped IN WET URINE…."

The class erupted into laughter, the teacher told me to go sit down, and this was the beginning of the REST of my time throughout high school.

Almost grasping the victory ring, always in sight … ALMOST.

I spent the rest of my high school career being an overachiever and knowing I didn't fit in. The harder I tried, the worse it got.

Yet somehow … all I wanted was to be loved and love others in return. Stupid shit, like the "wet t-shirt" contest I was in, never seemed to happen until I tried to force a result, or my ego got in the way.

At the time of writing this book, I'm 47 years old and have invested over half my life into being a business owner and entrepreneur. Saying that it is something I *do* misrepresents who I am and what I mean. Being an entrepreneur is not a job.

It is a way of life.

It is a mindset used to create versus waiting on something to be created.

It is a belief that if something must be done, and I understand what that is, then it is my responsibility to do it. This is extreme ownership and leads us to our very first lesson for life and business.

Core Values

You MUST know your personal core values. These values are your North Star for how you live your life. They are what's important to you and how you filter information.

It makes sense then to make sure that ANYONE you are considering being involved with on any significant level is in agreement with and honors your core values.

If you're a business owner, your core values are the MODUS OPERANDI for everyone's actions within your company.

It just so happens that my personal core values are also my companies' core values. This has allowed me to fully integrate what has earned me personal success and the functions of our companies that lead to scalability — without compromising individual or collective impact.

The Core Four

In our companies, my employees and I live by four core values; you should find yours, too. They become the foundation for every decision you make, every person you choose to align with, and most importantly, HOW you choose to see your VALUE in the world.

You don't need many; just as many as you feel adequately encompasses what's most important to you.

Here are mine, in order of importance:

- Integrity

- Information

- Innovation

- Income

Integrity is doing what you say when you say you'll do it, and if for whatever reason you don't fulfill that promise, going back, doing the work, and making it right.

Information is communication. It is the lifeblood of successful relationships and businesses. The clearer and more upfront we are when we communicate, in the timeliest of fashions with others, the more success we have.

Innovation applies to anything from technology to more efficient systems used to scale value for our clients. It is what we lean on.

Income is the fourth, last, and least important component of what we do. Yet, it is important enough to make sure people are rewarded according to the value they provide. As an entrepreneur, I'm in business to make money. I'm also in business to make sure that everyone attached to me makes what is commensurate to the value they put out into the world. My rule is that everyone on the team will win, or they're not allowed to be on the team.

You're Not Here to Be Average

I implemented my core values into my life because I refuse to be average. They are a tool I use to keep me grounded and on track to succeed. I can also weed out projects, people, and other elements of life and business because I can ensure that whatever I agree to do matches my core values.

Your core values have everything to do with refusing a life of mediocrity. You need to know what you stand for. You need to define what you want in excellence, so you don't settle.

**All my life, I have never considered myself average ...
Hell, my motto for the longest time was "Maximum Effort!"**

After getting through my teenage years, where I learned I was gifted in certain areas, I discovered the hard way what "average effort" gives me: a stomach full of cramps and a head full of regret.

There's nothing like being unprepared for a test by not studying correctly beforehand. I actually used to have nightmares about being in the middle of a test, knowing full-well I had ZERO ability to win. It always left me with the question, "Did I do EVERYTHING I could do to give myself the best chance of success?"

I remember when I was in my first semester of college, and my lack of a real work ethic caught up to me. I called my mom and told her of my fears of not winning and was hoping for her wisdom to help me get by. She simply said, "You can do anything for three months."

That sounded like work to me, and it held me accountable for my excuses. I didn't like it, so I decided that partying and girls were the BEST way to endure the pressure of keeping up with my classmates.

Life got so bad for a while that I actually tried really hard "fitting in" with people who didn't have the same life goals as me. I mean, I really tried being average. But over time, these people kicked me to the curb as hard as those who consistently practiced living in excellence. See, I didn't "fit in" anywhere because I hadn't identified WHO I was and what my values were. The moment the real me showed up instead of the one pandering to the group, I was ostracized.

It reminds me of the time I came home and told my parents I was solicited to be a model. Well, that's the edited, wishful thinking version of my story anyway. The truth is my buddy and I were walking in a mall in Springfield, Virginia. He was into martial arts and looked like a Greek god.

As we were leaving the food court, an older dude approached us and said to my buddy, "Do you have a second?"

He explained how he was always searching for "talent."

As soon as I heard those words, I thought …

I have talent.

He looked my buddy square in the eyes when he said, "This isn't a hoax. I take photos of all sorts of people, even a police officer. You can call him for a reference if you'd like."

My buddy didn't seem that interested, but I sure was. I saw it as a way of being GREAT. Being RECOGNIZED. Being RESPECTED.

So, when he was done pitching my buddy, I chimed in, "I'd like to give it a shot."

As we walked away with business cards in hand, my friend didn't seem that amused or flattered. Since he lived in the city, I believe now that it wasn't the first time he'd been approached by someone, so his defenses were up. But ... I could already see the headlines with me as the STAR.

The first thing I did when I got home was tell my parents.

My stepmom looked at me and said, "You're good-looking, just maybe NOT that good looking."

Damn, that stung. What she and I both didn't know at the time is that I would translate her words into "I'm not worthy of success."

Well, she was right; I'm no Fabio, ahem ... but I still look back on the attitude I got that day when she told me she didn't believe I could make it. When she said that, I heard "no."

Don't Tell Me "No"

I don't like people saying "no" to me.

Let me explain...

I love learning from others.

I love being given advice and can even take constructive criticism better than most.

But I HATE being told what to do.

Being told what to do doesn't work if we are shooting to be above average. If we're going to live in a world where we are our own bosses, and we aim to WIN, we have to set up some rules for propelling ourselves past average. Otherwise, the whole world will be our boss. And if you think giving it 95% effort is the same as giving 50%, you shouldn't even bother. If you think that when you hear "no," you should cave in, that's a problem. You will never reach your goals this way.

My Rules for Becoming ICONIC

#1. Burn the Ships

If you're going into business for yourself, it will require you to be MORE than you think. Get prepared by having a mindset that gives you NO OTHER OPTIONS. This helps you remain consistent when your mind is begging you to stop.

Over the course of my business life, I've seen many come and go in the entrepreneurial world. From a desperate entrepreneur who changes what they sell as often as most people change socks to others who are *almost* ready to sell their products and services but never pull the trigger.

Every time, their lack of success came down to having an easier path to take when the going got rough. Giving yourself no other option isn't a guarantee for success, but having too many options is a recipe for disaster because most people don't have the mental fortitude to continue working toward their goals when a reward doesn't come quickly enough.

#2. Set Your Vision

Have you ever heard that without vision, the people perish? If your dream is like a flashlight, how far and wide does that beam shine? Will you be able to see or light the way in the dark for others to see? When it comes to the vision you have for your money, would you prefer to invest it with someone who has a definite plan or with someone who's still figuring out whether their idea is what they really want to commit to?

#3. Set Your Foundation

What principles or values do you stand for? Without knowing the core values that you hold dear, you're susceptible to employees, vendors, and clients who are NOT who you serve best. When you know your values, they become a measure for everyone you allow into your space and money, whether they are bringing money or not.

#4. Create Your Playbook

If you want to scale ANYTHING profitably, it will require a step-by-step playbook for every operation within your company to consistently create the experience you desire everyone on your team (including clients) to have. I am known to always say (ask anyone I lead about this rule), "Sounds good. What does that look like if we multiply that idea x10 people or x100? Will it still work?"

#5. Execute the Play

One of the biggest hurdles I see MOST business owners struggle to overcome is "overwhelm." The cause of this is merely wearing too many hats in their business and not trusting others who are capable of doing certain tasks. In other words, they SUCK at delegation and invest too much time on tasks with little to no return.

Instead, figure out what you CAN'T delegate or what only you can bring to the table and enable others to do the tasks that are time wasters for you.

Once you implement these changes, you're in the process of being able to scale.

#6. Find Others Who Propel Your Vision-

One of the easiest ways to become complacent is to be the smartest person in the room.

You NEED to find people who are succeeding at a higher level than you. Not only will they increase your dreams and vision for your future, but they'll also answer questions and concerns that pop up … and … trust me, they *will* pop up.

#7. You Gotta Rest-

I know you're a badass and all, but all work, no play, and no rest will eventually make you an asshole. I tell you this from experience.

In my first business, I worked for eight years straight (Maximum Effort!) only to find after a week-long vacation in Florida that for at least six of those years, I was operating at 60% capacity.

Being a hard worker is par for the course when you consider doing your own thing, but remember, if you don't take a regular break, it'll be *you* who breaks.

Chapter 2

Living for the Moment

"Don't let yesterday use up too much of today."
—Unknown

For years I was motivated and moved "In the Moment."

You know, *the moment*, like AFTER you come out of the *Rocky* movie, shadow boxing, and chest-flexing; daring everyone ... ANYONE to step to you?

That moment that comes AFTER you leave the 2-day event with a headful of ideas convincing you that you're going to be rich, too, just like those beautiful, brilliant people on stage.

That moment the "deal" happens. When she says "Yes." Or your child is born.

I used to live *for* those moments, to live *in* those moments, and don't get me wrong, all we really have is NOW or a moment.

But there is a wrong way to live in the moment.

Without a solid plan or vision for your future, living "in the moment" is the coward's way of not dealing with reality. It's playing the victim.

I used to search for those moments like ol' Frank behind the barn when he was searching for that bottle of whiskey he hid from Ethel, desperately throwing shit around and getting angrier and angrier ...

Then, One Day, That Moment Found Me

I was about to learn that all those times I had been searching for those moments of exhilaration and ecstasy, I was actually teaching myself and whittling down to the essence of what I wanted in life.

That moment found me outside an Amway convention in Greensboro, North Carolina, 25 years ago.

Now, Amway has come and gone from my life, but THAT moment will NEVER go away.

It was the day I chose to accept a message of eternal hope and bend a knee to a leader who is stronger than me.

In front of 25,000 people, I was the first person to run from the stands and place myself in front of the speaker on stage to accept that I didn't know how to proceed alone.

I accepted Jesus into my heart.

Before I knew it, I found myself outside next to my car, and with the door open to hide me from prying eyes, I kneeled down and had a conversation with God.

I said, "I know I've just made an emotional decision to accept you into my life. I know that I'm going to mess up and let you go. Will you please never let go of me?"

As I was being ultimately vulnerable and sharing my deepest weakness with my Creator, I was willing to give up my biggest fear of being abandoned and ask that it wouldn't happen.

As fast as it happened, it was over. I walked back into the convention, not quite knowing what wheels I had set in motion.

Don't get me wrong, after the initial emotional high wore off:

I ran away from that moment.

I fought that moment.

I did my best to seek short-term pleasure in that moment.

The problem was every damn door I opened led me right back to THAT moment.

That moment of FREEDOM.

Freedom isn't free. That feeling that we're all looking for; accomplishment, recognition, wealth, fame, etc., requires a price to be paid.

I wanted ALL of that without having to do the REAL work to ensure I got it. This is when God gave me a taste of freedom and showed me the pathway to make sure I had enough integrity to keep it.

I did everything I could think of to negotiate within my mind to avoid having to endure the "pain" of growing up and taking responsibility for myself.

Freedom

Over the years, I have come to learn that freedom is not a birthright. Even if we have it today, it can be gone in an instant tomorrow.

Freedom ISN'T something to be sought after IN THE FUTURE; it's something to hold now.

It doesn't require me to be free from bondage to have it, either.

In fact, history is full of our heroes who, while going through the biggest struggles in life, found ways to dig deep, solidify their core beliefs, and bring forth a message that has forever shaped humankind.

Think of Dr. King Jr., Steve Jobs, Elon Musk … hell, even Edward Snowden. Do you think that Mother Teresa or Gandhi lived an easy existence? Yet each, in their own way, turned their personal stories of pain into an opportunity to share with the world a better way to live.

This freedom is found in KNOWING 100% what you're here to do and why you're doing it. When you are aware of this, you will never EVER quit on it.

There's freedom in the "pain of doing."

In doing the dirty work, the unpleasant work, and the hard work that NO ONE will ever see.

It's 4 am showers and pain-in-the-ass phone calls. It's holding yourself to integrity when someone isn't in theirs.

It's remembering to go for a damn walk, in the cold, when you don't have the right clothes or shoes, and having to talk to yourself the entire time that *this too shall pass.*

There's freedom in the "pain" of doing what's hard, in becoming the kind of person who revels in the "pain" and leans into it, instead of making up fu*cking excuses.

I don't have it all figured out, but I do have this:

I am a free man.

Free in my mind …

I know I OWN my mind.

Therefore … my body will surely follow.

I count on it and will continue to.

Learning to live in the moment is a "muscle" you develop, just like triceps or biceps. Unlike the gym, where you control when, how, and the length of the workout, living in the moment "workouts" often occur when you least expect them or want them.

When you've gotten amazing or horrible news, it's an opportunity to live in the moment.

Think about it. For most of us, when we hear great news, we celebrate for about 3 seconds, and then we're plotting what we're going to do with that "win."

When we hear frightening news, we often remember another time that felt the same way, and we go into "strategy" mode in order to do our best NOT to experience anything else that's painful.

Often, the BEST move is to just … be … still. In your MIND, that is.

For me, the real lesson of being in the moment is to be able to maintain focus on my definite major aim for whatever I'm joyful or fearful about. That is, to NOT allow exterior circumstances to dictate the clarity of my vision for the accomplishment of my goal(s).

I say this because, over the course of my life, I have come to the conclusion that I AM on the path I determined for myself, and the only person slowing me down from achieving it is me!

All of the "situations" that surface…these "moments" used to really mess with my head, my confidence, and my desire to continue to push forward.

It was like I was on the highway of life, and I kept taking every exit ramp I saw.

Living in the moment allows you to fully feel, observe, and choose a path because you go from reacting to responding in each situation.

Reactions tend to be old habits … that most likely will lead to results you're already familiar with.

Responding, on the other hand, allows you to CHOOSE which action (or lack thereof) to take.

Learning to live in the moment requires you to, well, live in the moment. You have to have the courage to allow the feelings of that moment to pass. Those feelings pass because you actually FEEL them and don't divert from them by going into action mode immediately.

Over time, with experience, you will learn to not react emotionally to everything that excites or scares you, and this is the moment where becoming ICONIC begins.

Chapter 3

Maximum Effort Will Fail You Every Single Time

A life best lived is a life by design. Not by accident, and not just by walking through the day careening from wall to wall and managing to survive. That's okay. But if you can start giving your life dimensions and design and color and objectives and purpose, the results can be staggering
—Jim Rohn

Everyone I know wants to live a life by design, but too many people want someone else to design it.

If you want proof, just look at social media. It's 2020, and people are bitching and moaning about the mask/no mask rules, having to stay at home, or being forced to work; they're griping about who's going to be president or how shitty our current one is doing.

One of my favorite sayings is "Maximum Effort." I've shared that with you a few times because it's stuck with me ever since I watched *Deadpool* with Ryan Reynolds, and I use it as an immediate pep talk for entering into a challenging situation.

Somehow, that two-word phrase allows me to immediately change my mindset into warrior mode. It does have its limits, and it's essential to know those limits when we're playing for keeps.

The First Time I Used It

In high school, I was on the JV team in tenth grade and played full-time on both the JV and varsity teams. I "sat the bench" watching the "big boys" play in varsity, being prepped for the following year. One day, the coach pointed to my teammate James running out to the centerfield position and addressed the rest of the team.

The coach said, "James isn't the best player in the outfield, hell, even on the team. Do you boys know why he plays every game?"

Silence among us newts.

"He plays every game because he hustles everywhere he goes."

When he told us that, all I could hear was "Maximum Effort."

It was a profound experience that I use to this day when my "I can't" is louder than my "I can."

The only problem is, eventually, you have to learn to respond in new ways to get new results, and if you're having trouble with that, go back and read the last chapter.

Turning Hustle into Muscle

One of the big secrets of real winners is that they do everything by design.

They are fully aware of the value of their time. They don't waste it, and they sure as hell won't let you destroy it.

Real winners use simple techniques with simple technology to be masters of their time.

The hardest lesson I've personally had to learn was time management.

Now, after coaching entrepreneurs for a while, I've learned I WAS NOT ALONE!

Let me share a story with you containing THREE TIPS to get ahold of your time and become INTENTIONAL with it:

When I shut my first business down in Virginia after 10-plus years and moved to New Hampshire, I found myself working for a design/build company in 2009.

By 2010, I was the top producer in the company and took a few liberties because of it. On Saturdays, if I was coming in to check emails, I'd wear my workout clothes. I thought since I was only in the back office and not in the retail space, it wouldn't matter.

NOPE. I had to have a meeting with the owner where I promised NOT to do that again.

I also arrived at company meetings either just on the button (7:30 a.m., or ten minutes later because the meetings didn't start on time ... EVER)

One day, the owner pulled me aside and said I needed to be in the meeting room at 7:30 or he was locking the door. I showed up at 7:35 and was locked out.

People in the room laughed as I knocked for a minute or two before going back to my cubicle, where I fumed the entire hour.

I mean, c'mon man ... I was only five minutes late! Why am I the one being targeted here?!?

I wish I could say that was my "aha" moment, but it wasn't.

Years later, Robyn, my wife, was busting my chops about being home late for dinner, or forgetting to text and make plans for the evening, etc.

I had the same attitude ...

"C'mon babe, if you had ANY IDEA how hard it is to keep this thing going, you'd be more forgiving like me."

I'd give myself a pass every single time because, honestly, I was scrambling.

That's another point, too.

How you do anything is how you do everything.

It wasn't just my timing with Robyn that was in chaos. My whole life was.

- I was trying to get paid on time by my clients.

- My employees and subcontractors were late.

- I was forgetting important AND necessary people to connect with to move my ideas forward.

- Being present with the people I cared about most was a struggle.

I could go on, but needless to say, I was constantly behind the eight ball in every aspect of my existence.

But here's where it hit home…!!

One day I was blathering on to Robyn about how little she understood about the pressure I was under—that being a few minutes late to dinner paled in comparison to keeping our finances flowing.

She then broke down what is required to get homework done for two children, craft a meal out of thin air, as well as make it in stages so that everything is hot at the same time.

She went on to explain how and why what she did kept the rest of the night flowing. By the end of her COUNSELING session, I realized that I treated her time as **LESS IMPORTANT THAN MY OWN.**

I also realized that getting Robyn and keeping Robyn are two totally different things. *How can I ask her to value me if I won't value her?*

How can I ask other people to respect my time if I don't?

Worse yet, in all those meetings that I allowed to go on and on and on ... I was teaching others my time wasn't valuable.

So, here's what I did, and I suggest you do the same.

NOW:

1. EVERYTHING GOES ON MY CALENDAR.

Personal texts to the family, business meetings, workouts, when I say everything ... I MEAN EVERYTHING.

2. TIME STUDY.

I learned from one of my mentors to do a two-week time study. I accounted in 15-minute increments what I did each day I was awake. (It's a pain in the ass to do, but totally worth it.)

3. KEEP MY COMMITMENTS.

If it's in my calendar and/or on my list, it gets done. Simple as that. I have reminders set up and notes that I can see in front of me to keep everything MOST important top-of-mind.

I do what I say I'm going to do, and when I slip, I make amends IMMEDIATELY.

The bottom line is that highly successful people focus on creating a maximum reward for the *effort* spent.

It's time to start living life by YOUR design and quit falling into a false narrative of conversations that have been created with a purpose to persuade you to support goals that may not help you accomplish your own. This can be on any subject, and the ones that come to mind are politics, religion, current social issues on race, sexuality — you name it!

When you make this change, maybe you'll start to see that engaging in another's rhetoric fulfills THEIR objectives and not your own.

Just remember that any fool can spot a problem; it takes a wise person to see a solution.

Chapter 4

Focus on Solutions

Opportunities are problems in search of solutions.
—Denis Waitley

What if I told you that allowing information into your head is like swallowing bait but speaking about it is like setting the hook?

The problem is that most people are fighting against things that don't really accomplish much. Win or lose; they don't get any closer to their goals.

The "bait" is the oversaturation of a mainstream message that goads us into believing you'll be happy if you just buy, do, have, or think ... XYZ.

You have this whole pond, lake, or ocean to eat in ... But you'd rather fight against a lure because the powers that be know human psychology well enough. If they just push their agenda or message out with the correct frequency, in a target-rich environment, with enough emotional influence, you'll eventually take the bait.

The "hook" is set the moment we begin to believe what's being said. We begin to believe mostly by allowing ourselves to repeat what we've heard to others.

Think about it for a minute. If you just take information in and do nothing with it, nothing really happens. Yet, all too often, once a message is heard with enough frequency, it's inevitable that it's going to be shared. With enough sources repeating the same message, bias sets in. Here's an example I bet you can relate to:

Have you ever listened to someone tell another person a "version of the truth" you know isn't factual?

Sure, you have.

Even days later, has the person who told the lie, had the nerve to come back to you and repeat it with 100% certainty?

Even if you take the time to "help to remember" facts about the real events, the original speaker of the lie will find ways to dodge, defend, or even turn the tables on you for confronting them.

This is a simple example of confirmation bias. The original speaker spoke, had an audience that listened, and from that interaction decided a desirable outcome ensued.

That desirable outcome became their truth, and therefore the lie that instigated it ALSO became a truth. Once this all sets in, it becomes very difficult for the person who told the lie to see any other version than the one they now believe in.

There are ways to pull yourself from the indoctrination of other's influences and CHOOSE your own thoughts.

Ask yourself:

Who are you, and what principles do you REALLY stand for?

What do you want to accomplish?

What aren't you willing to do to get what you want?

See how what I just suggested has EVERYTHING to do with you and nothing to do with anyone else?

We live in a world where the powers in control say they care about us when, in fact, their prime directive has little to do with us individually.

We codependently follow blindly and give our resources to others without a care in the world because they make us feel good. But these are only temporary solutions. This forces us to take quick wins and try to sustain between those wins.

We become addicted because the high of temporary wins is like eating a doughnut; it tastes good going down but isn't nourishing in the least.

We don't demand more concrete information because we aren't strong enough in our convictions to ask for it.

We don't demand more because we aren't doing what is required to create success, all because we haven't taken the time to define it for ourselves.

We don't demand it because it seems the price is too high to believe we're worth more, simply because we've been trained to think we're worth less.

Some people act like what we're going through is somehow unique in history. It isn't. It's a problem with our short-sighted, microwave popcorn society. Since the 1950s, our Western Society has mostly known abundance. Now that we're experiencing a little hardship, many people think that complaining about it on social media is somehow going to solve the problem.

The only thing that focusing on your problems brings is more problems.

You Have to Learn, "Energy flows where focus goes."

There's nothing quite like a keyboard warrior who is on a mission. They remind me of a fat-bellied uncle in the bleachers on Friday night at a football game, yelling and screaming at the coach or his nephew about playing the game. Sit down, bro ... just enjoy the spectacle. You are only here to be sold popcorn and sodas to anyway. Your opinion doesn't count because YOU have no effect on the outcome of the game.

Before you make that witty post, stirring up the mud, sit back and think for a minute, "Who is this serving, and what result do I want from it?"

In fact, since you've taken time to read this book, here are some things I've done that have helped me tremendously in achieving goals that were merely dreams when I began:

1. You can hire a coach.
2. Read books on the subject.
3. Join masterminds, where you can utilize "group think."
4. Write your goals out in so much detail you can actually feel what it's like to accomplish them.

The point is there is more than one way to get to your goals, yet there is ONLY one mindset that guarantees them: CERTAINTY.

So, how do you become certain about something you've never done before?

Here's a little story that might shed some light.

I was watching an online video where Jack Canfield, the *Chicken Soup for the Soul* guy, was saying how he made his first $100,000.

He didn't focus on HOW he would accomplish it; rather, he wrote down on a piece of paper that he would. He looked at it every day when he awoke and every night before he slept. Within one year, he had surpassed that income.

In another video I watched, Jim Carey, who got his start with "Ace Ventura, Pet Detective," speak on late-night television about a $10 million check he wrote to himself and kept in his wallet.

It was faded and worn, but he kept it there … and low and behold, his first commissioned check for Ace Ventura was $10 million.

I decided to give it a try. So, I went to the local store and picked up a 2'x3' green poster board. On it, I drew the Statue of Liberty in the middle, and in the four corners, I drew dollar signs and $1,000,000. This was my best representation of a million-dollar bill.

I set it on the nightstand beside my bed. Every morning, when I made the bed, as I did the well-known "air snap" for my comforter to gently fall back in place, it would blow the poster off the nightstand. I had to pick it up and place it back on the nightstand, ensuring that I glimpsed it daily.

At night, it would be the last thing I'd see before nodding off to sleep.

Within one year, my company went from $385,000 to $1,000,000.

I also learned a really valuable lesson about our subconscious minds. We MUST be specific in what we want because our subconscious mind will find the most efficient path to the result.

In this case, it was $1,000,000 gross. I should have been specific in my goal of $1,000,000 net profit…

Even though I was lazy and didn't focus with intention other than to look at the poster daily, it worked.

It will work for you, too, if you're just crazy enough to give it a try.

Chapter 5

Does Your Tenacity Match Your Capacity?

*Don't squander your potential living a life that amounts to
far less than the one you are capable of living.*
—Zero Dean

When your consistent efforts have refined your skills to a white-hot point,
and your dreams are unleashed to envision all you're capable of accomplishing
… you'll find the sacred zone where preparedness and opportunity meet.

***

Last night, I was talking to one of my great friends about Tom Brady.
We were discussing all the commentary about him going back to the
Championship Game of pro football.

Tom Brady has been to 47% of such events during his career.

Many people were commenting about him having natural gifts that
other people don't have. Others were pointing out the kind of coaching
he'd received and the types of teams he'd been placed on. What was in
common with all of this talk was that everybody had a defeatist attitude.

The conversation centered around how he got lucky, either by God or
circumstance. It wasn't because of Tom Brady.

Then our conversation went in a completely different direction.

We chatted about the fact that Tom Brady invests in practicing his
skill. He does the mundane things day in and day out and practices just
like everyone else.

We talked about how easy it'd be for Tom Brady to have his attention diverted from his purpose:

He certainly has enough to distract him: fame, fortune, the media, training on different teams, whatever it is, it could turn his head and take it out of the game.

But he wouldn't allow that.

Instead, Tom Brady gets up and acts like every day is game day. He builds up his muscles and mental and physical powers so that no matter what circumstance hits his life, he can perform.

Many of us are waiting on the big payday. We're waiting on "THE" opportunity to show up.

THE opportunity that will give us the riches and lifestyle we want. But deep down inside, we know we're not doing the work.

Deep down inside, we know we don't really deserve it. Not because we're undeserving people, but because we can't handle the pressure when it shows up.

And we haven't done the work to endure it.

Tom Brady is well-known as a winner because he can win when the going gets tough. He can be so mentally focused on the objective at hand that he will accomplish the task — no matter what's put in front of him.

That ability doesn't show up when he's making millions or winning Super Bowls. It didn't show up AFTER the fame started.

That ability is a mindset that began well before he was ever a champion.

My suggestion is if you believe in who you are and the value you know you can bring ... then practice that value every single day.

Practice that value, even when you won't get paid for it, when you get getting ridiculed for it, and when you get ripped off because of it.

Practice that value no matter what.

Do this, and I know you will win the day…

I don't know when it'll happen. I don't know where it'll happen. And I certainly don't know how it'll happen. But it will happen.

Practice that value, and the opportunities will show up. Then because you've put in the work, you will be prepared for those opportunities. You, like Tom Brady, will turn on your mental toughness, and you *will* win the day.

Chapter 6

What Kind of Man Are You?

The only person you are destined to
become is the person you decide to be.
—Ralph Waldo Emerson

Are you the kind of man who would throw trash out your car window?

Are you the kind of man who'd watch someone drop their wallet in the parking lot and quickly look around to see if you could grab it yourself?

Are you the kind of man who would take advantage of MY daughter if she'd had a little too much to drink and needed a "friend"?

No?

Then why in the hell aren't you willing to treat yourself with the same respect?

Why aren't you the kind of man who leads by example?

Why do you keep making excuses by blaming your wife for your bullshit attitude?

Why do you keep making promises to fix the trim in the basement but then forget to schedule it in your calendar, so you don't forget?

Why do you keep looking at porn?

Worse yet, why are you lusting after that girl who works in the building next to you? All it does is make you ignore the woman at home who's given her entire life to you.

45

Why do you keep sneaking that drink before you come home and then upping the ante just because your spouse pretends alongside you that you're completely sober?

Why do you listen to her until the phone rings or notifies you that someone responded to your social media post? Then you literally turn your head, so 100% of your attention goes to your own ego?

That's a lot of questions, but not so many answers.

That's my point.

When you were a kid, the authorities in your life gave you the questions, and you had to come up with the answers.

Now that you're all grown up, it's your job to realize the answers are available everywhere, but you're required to come up with the right questions.

Being a "real" man comes down to whether you're going to give yourself permission to be a boss or a bitch.

Sure, you can raise your voice and flex your muscles to intimidate someone else BUT YOU'LL STILL be a bitch.

That'll work for you until you meet a boss.

That'll work until you meet a man who's willing to die for his cause.

All that bravado works for people who are also uncertain and bullies. Yet it is seen for the weak-ass chest-thumping it truly is to a man in the ring.

That's because the man in the ring has already made a commitment to fight the real enemy.

The man in the ring cuts through all the drama and noise to focus on making an IMPACT.

He's learned to quiet the voice in his head that won't lead to victory.

He's learned to define victory by overcoming his justifications and replacing them with integrity.

He's learned that victory includes staying the course because his word to others matters, even if it looks like he won't win for his efforts.

The man in the ring has learned to kill his ego, assess his weaknesses, and do what's hard consistently, with joy, to have an "easy" life.

The man in the ring has the left-right combos to knock his enemy out and knows he's put in the work to outlast his opponent if required.

While that man listens to the bitch outside the ring complaining about why he won't take the shot, he knows that's just noise from the peanut gallery ...

It's just another distraction from victory.

If you want respect, you have to start treating yourself with it first.

Respect yourself enough to know that...

Everything happens FOR you, not TO you. Everything happens at exactly the right moment, neither too soon nor too late. You don't have to like it ... it's just easier if you do.
—Byron Katie

Learn to use every experience as a mirror instead of licking your wounds and feeling sorry for yourself.

Only you know those thoughts that keep you from daring to be great.

Only you know what kind of man you really are ...

So, what kind of man are you?

Are you willing to get in the ring, or are you going to stay on the sidelines cheering the real warriors on?

I made my choice, but it took some time for me to implement the ACTIONS I needed to so I could become the kind of man. I wanted. I'm the kind of guy who wants to start with the foundation first. It doesn't make sense to me to put a roof on before the walls go up.

I had to take a little more time to understand what's most important and what's not.

With all the information out there that promises to make our dreams come true, it's becoming MORE and MORE difficult to know what actions lead to the MOST effective and efficient results too.

There's That Question Again

It's why you MUST answer "What do YOU really want?" as you are considering an action to take. Once you know what you really want, it becomes easier to understand what you have to do to get to the goal.

It becomes easier to see where you're falling short of the "ideal." It becomes easier to identify habits that take away from the confidence of owning who you really are, what you're meant to do, and more importantly, HOW you can find a repeatable set of steps so you can scale them to produce the outcome you truly desire.

Once you begin to see where you want to be and where you are, then you can make a choice about if you will remain stuck in the habits that aren't serving you. It also becomes easier to let those habits go so you can move from living a good life into living a GREAT life.

You may not see the benefits of your new choices for a little while, but your increased self-worth by letting go of what doesn't serve your ideal life will carry you through until you do.

I've made my choice ... have you?

Chapter 7

Mastering the Monotony

*Boredom is, therefore, a vital problem for the moralist since
at least half the sins of mankind are caused by the fear of it.*
—*Bertrand Russell*

Life's all about duality. It resembles the saying that "Freedom isn't free."

For you to live a life of freedom, at least here in the US, someone else has to sacrifice their time and sometimes their life to ensure you have the right to live, speak, and go where you want.

When it comes to your health, to live a life free of significant pain and disease, you have to be willing to put yourself through physical exercise that can range from uncomfortable to downright painful.

The same goes for work. For you to have the freedom of money and time, you often have to give up both to pursue THAT American dream as well.

And just because you're free to pursue it doesn't mean you'll find it. In fact, most fail in their pursuit.

Entering the Winner's Circle

Over the last two decades, I've made it my mission to fully understand why most fail and how I could avoid the same fate.

I've also found the foundational building blocks required to ensure my success (as I define it).

For me, success is defined as wealth, health, and doing what I want with who I want, when I want.

I've found it; I live it, and you can, too. There is only one main philosophy you have to live by and that you must measure every decision by. There's only one habit to adopt to find yourself in the winner's circle of life.

That's INTEGRITY.

Integrity simply means doing what you said when you said you'd do it. It means if you mess up, that you make it right ... Period.

There are so many reasons to live in integrity. The main one is that when you habituate it, you begin to believe in yourself. That's right; you simply start to believe your thoughts, words, and actions. Then when you create new and audacious goals, you will believe that you have what it takes to accomplish them because you always do what you say.

You also need to make sure that you measure every decision by making sure your potential choice aligns with who you are and what you believe.

This means you have to understand why you're here, what your core values are, and what you believe your life story is all about.

When you can separate yourself from the drama you're in and take a 50,000-foot view of your life; you can see if choice A or B is directing you toward YOUR integrity or away from it.

Learning how to do this takes time.

We have to experiment with the process and get used to it. Give yourself a break if you mess up. As long as you're living, you have time to correct just about anything.

Mastering Monotony

There's only one habit you need to practice to live a life of freedom and integrity — however you define it.

You must learn to become a *Master of Monotony*.

A healthy body, a strong mind, and a successful life are built on repetition. And 95% of these activities aren't glamorous either. When you see a dude with muscles in his forehead, just know it isn't the sports drink he's paid to endorse that got him there. No, he's put in years of exercise, day in and day out.

Even though he looks the way he does now, there were days when he felt like going to the gym and days he didn't. On some days, he was likely sick, tired, and fighting with his ex or partner. But he still went and kept his commitment to himself even on those days when everything was against him and trying to prevent him from going.

He did it anyway because he'd mastered the monotony. Even though he had a choice, he took the option of not going off the table and kept moving toward the promise he made to himself.

Quit looking for a shortcut to your dreams.
Decide NOW is the time that you'll pay the full price.

When you do this, you will join the company of other champions who, just like you, have chosen to live in integrity, who understand their purpose here on earth, and who refuse to allow their "bitch voice" to win ...

Do what's hard to you so that you can live easy knowing you're up for whatever gets thrown your way.

A Hard Cut

I remember when I was cut from the college baseball team like it was yesterday.

When I attempted to throw a ball from centerfield to home, it didn't even make it in the air to second base.

The culprit was major tendonitis in my shoulder, and on a gorgeous spring day, after 13 years of mastering the monotony of baseball — it was over.

When that happened, I thought I was over, too. Baseball was the only reason I'd gone to college … well, that and girls.

In an instant, I was lost at sea without any land in sight. Little did I know that THIS was one of those defining moments in life.

After that day, I struggled for another six years until I found something as important as baseball to sink my teeth into.

Choosing to open a service-based business gave me unlimited opportunity for refinement, self-growth, and the freedom to succeed.

I could take the same mindset for playing baseball, "Maximum Effort," and will my business into paying our bills.

Mastering More Than the Monotony

There are so many painful lessons I've had to master, some I know, I'll still have to master.

But through learning to be patient, trusting the process, and doing the mundane work, I've learned to teach others on my team a "better way" to do the same. Because of this, I have been able to literally fire myself from specific tasks and grow our companies.

What is Your Real Intention?

No one I know, would tell me, "I want to be average."

NO ONE would tell me, "I'm just here to participate."

It's become automatic for people to tell me that they are working for greatness on some level.

I mean, no one I talk to is stupid, so they know what to say when I ask them what their intention is.

As for others … their mouth will start moving before their brain has caught up …

I don't blame them. Hell … I used to be exactly the same.

One day though, enough was enough

I was sick and tired of being "better than most."

I was f'in done with the YO-YO of temporarily winning, only to lose it all again and start over.

I was angry at EVERYONE around me.

Half-ass efforts and half-ass results.

Everyone had an excuse, AND everyone ALWAYS bailed when the "SHIT HIT THE FAN."

Oh, everyone was a damn fan-boy as long as we were winning. But everyone found a way to leave and leave me with a mountain of buffalo dung to sift through so I could claw my way to being "great" again.

It's a damn roller coaster of emotions and a ton of focused effort to get your equilibrium back EVERY DAMN TIME YOUR BELL GETS RUNG!

Being the hard-headed dude I am, I finally started asking myself the REAL questions. They led me to the only real one that matters:

"Kris, what is your REAL intention?"

What I found out when I forced myself to answer it was kind of embarrassing

What I really wanted was to START something and then coast my way to success. I wanted everyone else to do the day in, day out, monotonous work while I lived the "HIGHLIGHT" reel.

I began to see that EVERYONE I was attracting around me was living the **EXACT SAME LIE**. I had also attracted to me ... people who were EXACTLY LIKE ME.

So, here are three tips if you're experiencing the yo-yo, have made a choice to go "all in," and/or want to live an UNSTOPPABLE LIFE:

1. Who you surround yourself with is EVERYTHING

You can find a lot of information out there to figure out who's your group. "Who's your group" is another one of those clichés, but WAY too many people don't ever take the time to answer the question.

If YOU really want to win over the long haul ... you MUST put people in your life who will push you.

In today's society of polite bullshit, we're lifting up creampuffs because they're politically correct.

We DON'T HAVE HEROES ANYMORE!!

The media doesn't focus on people who are constantly striving to live each day with intentionality and purpose. We are standing in the gap between what society now deems acceptable and what it TAKES TO GET THE REAL WORK DONE. That doesn't mean the strivers aren't there.

What's AMAZING is that once you REALLY choose to be unstoppable, it's almost as if by magic, the same kind of people start popping into your life.

You'll also probably have to make some tough decisions about who's in your circle now ... but that TOO takes care of itself if you are really in it 100%.

2. Commit to DOING the HARD WORK

You may not like this, but here's the truth. The rest of your life is going to require HARD, sometimes boring, sometimes scary-as-shit, hard friggin' work.

Not sometimes ... **every damn day.**

That doesn't mean you won't enjoy it, or your life either. It simply means that you must understand and commit to NEVER being a victim again.

It isn't anyone else's fault that your milk spilled, or you are treated unfairly. IT'S JUST PART OF THE HARD WORK OF GROWTH.

Embrace it. Hold onto the discipline of that mindset, with what it ACTUALLY takes to win. Do that, and it will set you free.

It will also take away that feeling of "something's missing" in your life because you will BE IN PURPOSE ON PURPOSE!

You will use the "wins and losses" as a measuring stick, not a defining MOMENT in your life.

When you're training every day, you're bound to win and lose. Celebrate the wins and learn from the losses. If you have breath tomorrow, it's just another OPPORTUNITY to do the work again.

3. Dream Bigger and Take the Damn Shot!

I promise you that as you are FULLY committed to living an unstoppable lifestyle, you are going to get a little salty. Your tolerance for other people's BS is going to grow thin.

Your tolerance for YOUR BS will grow thin, too!

You'll be confronted with your limiting beliefs. You'll see where you AREN'T going all in. You'll find yourself wanting to be RADICALLY HONEST with yourself and other people. You'll seek out clarity in every conversation that's in your head, that messes with your gut instincts and diverts you from a path you know is true in your heart.

You'll eventually see that IF you're willing to do whatever it takes, why wouldn't you attach a goal worthy of that effort? Your new group will be doing the same thing ... and guess what??

You'll then DO the same things successful people do, and begin to have the same results they've achieved.

You'll simply believe that YOU ARE WORTHY of more ... all because you are committed to more.

Damn, am I passionate about seeing people win. I'm committed.

The question is ... **ARE YOU?**

Chapter 8

Your Vision, Your Values, and Your Verdict

If you aren't going all the way, why go at all?
—Joe Namath

You need a vision for what it is you're trying to accomplish. It doesn't matter whether you're working in a job or are running a business. It doesn't matter if you are thinking of your personal life. If you don't have a vision for your family or finances, and you don't have an eye for what you want your life to look like, you'll eventually find yourself accepting a lot less than you deserve. The trap here is that MOST people shrink their goals to the reality they're living instead of changing the reality (work) to match their lofty goals.

The truth is if we aspire to live life to its fullest, we need a vision. Although your vision might begin as small and harder to see, as you fan that flame, your picture will get more significant.

Developing your business starts with incorporating your values. Those values will end up becoming your core values. If your business' core values are everything that you stand by, your verdict is simply your personal decision to go "all in" on your vision and core values.

It's the one area that you must refuse to compromise. It's the one decision you'll never again have to question, only your adherence to it. This is how you grow!

Developing a Personal Vision

When one of our kids started dating somebody recently, they asked if they could bring this new person home with them to sleep in the same bed.

My wife Robyn and I were talking about it, and she said, "It just doesn't quite feel right in my gut."

As I listened, I thought about the vision we have as a family.

When I moved up to New England in 2009, Robyn and I didn't have sleepovers for over eight years because she had young kids in the home.

I remember getting on the phone with some of my buddies around the five or six-year mark, and they would say: "Dude, do you know how much money you guys not living together is costing you?" and "I wouldn't stay with a girl if, after five years, she didn't want to sleep in the same bed as me."

I replied, "Yeah, life would be so much easier if we combined our incomes and did everything together, but she has a personal boundary. Even though I don't fully agree with her, I trust her judgment with her ethics and morals."

To help Robyn find a solution to what to say to her son about sleeping with his girlfriend in our home, I asked her questions and drew out her feelings.

I reminded her that one of our other kids had been dating somebody for about four years, and we hadn't let them sleep together yet. I told her that just because they're in college now, and they're 18, doing their own thing, doesn't mean that our rules change.

As we continued talking, I asked Robyn, "What's the reason that you didn't want us to sleep together and let the children know that we were a couple?"

The reason we had decided to wait to sleep in the same bed with the kids around was the same reason that applied to our current situation. We reasoned that even though the kids were getting older, they were not fully adults yet, and they still needed us to carve a path for them. They needed us to show them what was right and wrong in life.

Robyn was concerned that if we didn't allow the kid to stay in the same bed, that somehow, someway, our kid might not want to spend as much time with us.

Despite that, allowing the two kids in the same bed wasn't resonating with her because it was going against her values. As we explored the topic more, we found out what those values were.

I said, "Let's say they're dating that person, and it's a fairly new relationship — which it is — and they sleep in the same bed. Well, the next thing you know, if they break up with that person and start dating someone else, they will want to bring them home to sleep in the bed, too. We don't live in a brothel."

If I were the parent solely in charge, I would allow it to happen one time, but it better be with that person that they're willing to make a commitment to for the rest of their life.

The way I looked at it was that it wasn't just about sleeping in the same bed. We know that 18-year-olds are going to do what 18-year-olds do.

What was at stake was:

What do I condone?

What does it do to the relationship to take it to that next level?

What am I willing to allow in my house, whether good or bad?

We had to keep in mind that this would become a slippery slope over time.

Here's a scenario: first, you start buying your kids' drinks. Then they're bringing the drinks to you. After that, your 15-year-old is drinking alcohol, smoking weed, or doing whatever else regularly.

Do you see what you started?
It's hard to close the door on that.

What is it that we're really trying to teach our kids?

What values do we really live by?

I didn't always have those values. Back when I was a different guy, the decision we were weighing about the kids wouldn't have made much sense to me. Now, I had to honor Robyn's values if I wanted to stay in our relationship. By respecting Robyn's values, I focused on what I brought instead of what I received. I started to realize the real commitment that I would need to make in my relationship with her to move our vision forward.

It's a funny thing to go from "my" vision to "our" vision. It required a level of vulnerability for me that I had to grow into. In fact, I found out that I didn't trust people inside of an intimate relationship.

This was definitely a personal development moment for me, and it began with such a simple phrase uttered by Robyn. She simply said one day, "You're my best friend."

I don't know about you, but I'd invested years in this woman's life. I had sacrificed more than I thought I ever would for another human being, with little understanding of the ROI I was receiving. Have you ever felt the same way? Let me tell you another story to help you understand.

> **The reason what Robyn said hit me right between the eyes is that my first wife had said those same words to me the day I looked her in the eyes and said, "I don't want to be married to you anymore."**

The way my ex said it that day was different, though. It was after I'd said "We're through" that she began to cry. In a tearful voice soaked in exasperation, she said, "But I'm losing my best friend."

Yes, it hurt to see her hurt.

Yes, I have a natural inclination to be a hero and make things better when I can.

No, it was NOT the time to say that. We'd had over ten years for her to have real talks with me, be vulnerable, and share HER vision of why I was so important in her life. It was only AFTER the fact that she chose to be vulnerable.

On the contrary, it was a simple day during the summer, in the driveway after work, when Robyn uttered those startling words. Nothing spectacular nor emotional elicited such a response. Robyn simply looked at me in June of 2018 and said with a smile on her face, "You're my best friend."

All my hard work, all the years of feeling unappreciated from her (and maybe everyone else, too) had been recognized and boiled down to a simple phrase.

I hadn't set the stage for the compliment. I hadn't manipulated, cajoled, harassed, or even asked. It just showed up.

> **From that day, I began to take my eyes off "my" vision.**

I began to do the hard work of hearing what is being said, and I began to incorporate her vision and my vision into our vision for the future.

This experience in dichotomy has allowed me to see the same in most people who are struggling and trying to find their success, especially in business. See, they get their heart all set on something, and it feels right, fun, and exciting.

They go after it, and then they realize all the hard work required to make it happen.

**Since it's not their purpose, and just their passion;
they eventually don't feel like doing it anymore.**

Just like in an intimate relationship, they may become reactionary instead of intentional — slowly slipping into the victimhood of someone who is NOT in control of their future.

I realized something a long time ago — that if I have a choice between what my heart and gut tell me to do, I'm better served when I follow my gut every single time.

I want to pass that information along to you because I know that you might be struggling with a few questions:

"What is my purpose?"

"What am I on earth to do?"

"What tough decisions do I need to make?"

"Is my heart telling me the right thing to do, or do I listen to that little voice inside me?"

That little voice nags and says, "Man, I might have to go against the grain, I might have to do something different, I might have to become something different." This is where you MUST begin to listen to your gut. My personal experience in coaching people over the long haul is that we eventually make choices that align with our gut anyway. Those who choose to never listen to their gut create endless drama.

There have probably been many times in our lives that we can look back on where we followed our hearts and not our guts. When we do that, we can probably also see that we ended up having to clean up a mess because we made the wrong choice.

When you are at a crossroads and can't detect your gut, I want to help you through that.

Develop and Depend on Your Vision

Understand before we go any further (and there is a reason I am repeating this), you need to have a vision. You need to have a dream so big that it actually scares you a little bit. If it doesn't scare you so that you don't know how you're going to accomplish that vision, I want to challenge you to believe that you might not have a big enough idea … yet.

> **As you're developing your vision, think about who you are as a person, what values you carry, and what's most important to you.**

The answers to these questions will become your core values. You can use them in how you live your life and who you're willing to interact with. You can use them in business, whether with customers and employees — internal or external. It doesn't matter.

Don't Stand Down

Finally, I want to let you know something. You're going to face challenges that will make it extremely difficult to know which decision to make. When you get to those challenges requiring you to choose between what your heart desires and what your gut's telling you do, allow me to suggest that your gut is rarely wrong.

To conclude our story regarding the two kids and one bed, Robyn ended up reaching out to our kid via text and letting him know that she just wasn't comfortable with the sleeping arrangement. He texted back: "Can you tell me why you came to that conclusion?"

She glanced over at me with an expression like, "What do I say?" As she started typing out a long message to him, I said, "Listen, all you need to tell him is this is what your decision is, and if he wants to know more, you can get on the phone and talk about it."

That settled it.

As of this writing, they're still coming this weekend and will be sleeping in different bedrooms, but everything's okay.

We made the right decision, but if we hadn't, Robyn would have had to wrestle with a choice she didn't like. If you don't stick by your core values and what you truly want, you will wrestle with some things that you don't like, either.

But when your vision and values are strong enough, you can lean into your intuition and trust what it's telling you.

Chapter 9

Slaying Your Superman Syndrome

If you are feeling inadequate, worthless,
or NOT ENOUGH, you didn't get those ideas from God.
—Lisa Bevere

Have you ever gone to a networking event or function, and as you observed the people around you, felt inadequate?

From where you're standing, it might seem like everyone in the room is either killing it, making money, has the most beautiful significant other, or that they live on a much higher level than you.

When I first started surrounding myself with "winners," I felt like I was wearing a "shit-suit" and stood there waiting for someone to point out that I was "THAT" smell in the room. When I thought that way, it would throw me completely off my game. I could feel the confidence leaving my body, and I counted the seconds on the clock until I could leave.

At the very least, I would take my place in the crowd and do my best to blend in while secretly wondering *what on earth do these Alphas have that I don't?*

Was it luck?

Had they made choices earlier in their life that had led them to this state of power, influence, and being in control of themselves and the room?

Maybe they had just been "gifted" with a superhuman ability to be social butterflies?

Well, I'm here to tell you those kinds of people are the exception, NOT the norm.

We Are All the Same

After coaching top-level athletes, business moguls, thought leaders, and influencers ... I can tell you that these successful people STILL have the same fears we all do. They still make mistakes, call shots that miss, and sometimes look foolish in the process.

It is true, however, that their self-image is healthy.

It's also true that they have something extra ...

Here's a hint: they care more about what it is they're called to do than what you think about it.

That's because they have a purpose.

They feel the fear and do it anyway.

There is no exact formula to their success except they've invested time in getting definite about what they are doing, why they're doing it, and the outcome they expect from it.

From that small choice comes confidence.

It's not that they have the confidence they'll nail it in front of you ... rather, they have the belief that they won't quit no matter WHAT YOU OR ANYONE ELSE THINKS.

These titans are willing to do whatever is necessary to get where they want to go, and they will face any fear to realize their objective.

Their focus is palpable because so few people actually know what they want. That's the "extra sauce" everyone can feel just by surrounding themselves with people who are intentional with their lives.

We often judge others on how we perceive them winning and measure it against our losses.

We don't think about their struggles.

We don't think about their fears.

We don't consider the problems they have because THEY aren't focused on their issues ... they're focused on solutions.

You need to know that your fear of being inadequate is just as powerful of a demon to the highly successful as it is to someone who's just starting out.

NONE of us have accomplished what we've never accomplished ... yet.

The difference is that winners just won't quit.

They're willing to get their ass back up after a catastrophic loss, dust themselves off, and call the shot again.

Powerful people are willing to stand with their fears, quiet their minds, and do what's necessary to reframe to improve.

So, the next time you want to hero-worship, consider that you might just be lowering your opinion of yourself. There's a difference between acknowledging someone's achievements and putting someone on a pedestal. Hero-worshiping creates the illusion that they have achieved something you cannot.

It's disempowering and allows you to make an excuse not to give life your best effort. Hero-worship is a wolf of self-limiting beliefs disguised in the perceived social etiquette of sheep's clothing. In other words, it's a dead giveaway that YOU aren't who you pretend to be in front of others.

If you fall for the flattery, you have work to do because your ego is being fed.

If you're the one giving it, you have work to do because your ego craves the attention you're giving so freely.

Remember:

The ONLY thing that's different between a superhero and a loser is that a superhero is willing to FACE the enemy ...

The real question is ...

Are you?

Chapter 10

Relationships Are the New Reward

A great relationship is about two things: first, appreciating the similarities and second, respecting the differences.
—Unknown

I can't tell you how many times I've been out with young bucks, who have bragged about the beautiful girls they've "slain."

Or how often I've had to sit and listen to them tell me about the "killer" account they've landed, how much they sold last month, or the new sports car they just bought to reward themselves for kicking so much ass.

When I was younger, that kind of stuff used to impress me. I mean, who doesn't want to go home with the most beautiful girl at the bar? Who doesn't want to have a fantastic month in sales or feel the power of 500 horses begging you to let them loose on the streets?

It sounds tempting.

But as I've grown in business and grown UP in life, I've changed what impresses me.

The Truth About Commitment

See, that gorgeous girl or guy?

He or she is usually one of the most insecure people around ... and if you're going to keep 'em around, you're going to have to be the REAL deal. If you're a guy, you'll need to deal with other men who continually infringe on your territory. And you'll have to commit to embracing her less desirable traits because NO ONE is perfect ...

You'll have to fight sometimes, too. That's my point.

It's easy to say the magic words one night and get the girl. It's easy to win a single account, have a killer month, or get a cool toy.

It's hard to keep her. It's hard to maintain that fantastic client, rack up month after month of great sales, and afford that expensive luxury car.

If you want to win consistently, it requires commitment.

Are You Using Personal Integrity?

People screw up their integrity all the time. They are so committed to that girl or client that they forget their most important priority: their personal integrity. Personal integrity is being true to yourself. It's like they say on the airplane before takeoff, "Put on your own mask before you assist someone else."

Until you have a great relationship with yourself, you will have a tough time creating and sustaining quality in the relationships around you.

You'll go left when you should go right.

You'll speak when you should listen.

You'll offer shitty advice because you don't have the ability to draw from valuable experiences.

**We all love to live by our intentions,
but we all judge others by their actions.**

We love to remember everything "good" we've done and downplay the negatives.

We are only as strong as the areas where we're most susceptible to fail. Life has a way of poking holes into us until it finds where we're weakest. The fairytale is that we CAN live happily ever after. That somehow, we … arrive. I'm here to suggest that you will NEVER "arrive." That idea is just another of the paradigms we've been sold as a collective so that we don't continue to do the work required to live a life of excellence.

We are judged by our weakest link. Everyone is so used to being sold on benefits instead of authenticity that we tend to look for ways to bring someone winning back down to earth. People also look for a lack of integrity as a way to discredit successful people because if they can find it, the pressure is relieved for them individually to possibly have to commit to a higher standard.

Real, sustainable success isn't a place you arrive at.

Real success is the lifestyle you live by daily.

All you ever have to do to see how much success you really have is gauge the quality of your relationships.

If you're running alone, and you feel lonely, you have some real work to do. This is your opportunity to get vulnerable. This is your opportunity to live authentically and bravely in a world that wants you to conform.

You may get lucky and find someone or a group to relate to, but that's not likely. A better way is to find the courage to commit to discovering YOU and to be willing to boldly share your gifts with anyone who crosses your path.

Adapting to Change

In 2006, I realized that something was happening in the economy. Clients who had said they would work with us were hesitating. Although our track record was eight years of keeping our doors open, everything was about to change.

By 2009, I had to close my business down, and I was over $300,000 in debt. As I was shutting down my company that I thought I would have for the rest of my life; I could see my dreams slip away. I became more fearful than I'd ever been. I got more frustrated with my relationships.

Because we lived in rural Virginia, most of my relationships revolved around family and very close friends. This was a time when social media was just becoming mainstream. My business required so much of my time that I didn't focus on making friends or being intentional about who I invested time with. I realized that my close relationships were strangling me and keeping me from becoming who I needed to become ... who I felt *led* to become.

So, with a heavy heart, in 2009, I closed my business, got divorced, and moved 1,000 miles away from anyone and everything I knew. It was the scariest action I'd ever taken in my life. When I left, I knew I would have to forge new relationships.

I got a job in New Hampshire with a home remodeling company for a small amount of time. I had decided to become a model employee and do everything in my power to build a career within this organization. Within a year of being there, I saw that my income was limited, and in my off time, I researched this new trend called the internet and social media. Then I reached out to influencers hoping to find information that would help unlock the keys of where I wanted to go in life.

That's when I found my first mentor, who eventually became my business partner. Since that time, I have never stopped looking for relationships with people who are where I want to be in life.

Follow the Clues

I now understand that the people who have already accomplished what I want can teach me how to get where I want to go quicker.

In developing these relationships, the one thing that I started to understand is that value is a two-way street. Now, to most of us, value is received in the form of money. But there are many, many, many ways to offer value to people who have the knowledge you want.

Don't let your lack of funds be the reason that you stay stuck.

Of everything I've written, this is the most important takeaway: *the circle of people you surround yourself with will have the most significant impact not only on your income but on your quality of life.*

Another way of saying it is that *who you're aligned with matters more than what you do.*

Chapter 11

What Master Do You Really Serve?

Always remember, your focus determines your reality.
—George Lucas

You probably know the story of the two wolves. One wolf on your left shoulder is the good wolf, helping you accomplish your goals, and the other wolf on your right shoulder leads you to destruction.

The question is, which one wins in the end?

Answer: the one you feed.

Although it makes a ton of sense, enough for a third grader to understand, most of us still act like toddlers when it comes to applying such a powerful principle in our lives.

When everything is going well, we boast about our success, how amazing life is, and with a little EXTRA swagger in our step, we walk around like we have life by the balls.

Yet, when the shit hits the fan, that swagger turns into weak knees, and hiding from those you're afraid will judge you. That's when all sorts of "bad" habits start showing up.

Do you want to learn how to NEVER have that happen again?

Feeding the Wolf

The further I climb up the "mountain" of life, the clearer I see.

What used to boggle my mind now appears as simple, clear, and direct answers telling me how to win.

Complicated challenges in my life, even my emotions — which used to stop me in my tracks — now can't hide the solutions that I can deploy at a moment's notice to help me accomplish my goals.

I want you to have the same level of clarity as I do because I remember how BADLY I wanted to win and how very hard it was to get any traction toward my goals.

I bet you want to win, too. But if you're repeating experiences that tell you you're not progressing, it's because you're feeding the wrong damn wolf, PERIOD.

The first thing you have to do to really start winning at life is simply choose which "wolf" to feed. Are you going to feed the wolf of negativity or positivity? Are you going to look at life as happening to you or for you? Once you make this basic choice, you'll be able to wrestle with disempowering thoughts when they arise. It might not seem like you're making headway toward your goals, but I promise you that you're tilling the field of opportunity and making sure it's fertile.

You have to know with clarity where you want to be, what you want to accomplish, and what it will feel like to win at your desired outcome.

This doesn't mean waiting around until the opportunity or timing is right because imperfect action beats perfect non-action every time.

Along your journey toward achieving your goals, you'll start to get clearer and clearer on EXACTLY what that end goal looks like. Keep it in the front of your mind so you won't miss it.

Like I've said before, this means that you will have to draw a line in the concrete and decide on some basic rules that you will live by, NO MATTER WHAT. These will become your personal core values, so make sure they really mean something to you.

The second thing that you must do to win and keep the streak going, is apply your core values to every situation you find yourself in.

Of course, the "easy" or "feel-good" situations will be a breeze.

You will want to use the momentum you've created with your easy wins to lean into the conditions that try to knock you out of your seat.

When you're slapped in the face by a challenging situation, CHOOSE to be still, find your center, and calm your ass down.

Take the time to assess these circumstances with your rational, core values-based thinking instead of your reactionary, emotional mind.

Once you get some clarity, you can then *respond* to your situations instead of reacting. The outcome is almost always guaranteed to be better for your long-term success.

Win Big

Finally, if you want to win ... and win big, you must keep going and #dothework no matter what.

You must know that life will never be an "easy street." People who think that life will get easier are weak because they believe the lie. They want to know that growth and success mean they'll never struggle again.

Quite the opposite is true.

Life will get harder for many reasons, but you will simply get better.

The only way to know what master you serve is when you're in the middle of your shit. This is the only time that you can genuinely experience who you are, what you're made of, and what choices you will make in the heat of battle.

If you take time to solidify your habits and responses during peacetime, you won't bleed as much during the wars of your life.

If you let off the pedal when it's easy, I promise you'll be passed by others continually looking for a lane that ensures their victory.

So ... What master are you going to serve?

You don't have to tell me.

It'll be apparent by the words that leave your lips and the actions you take (or don't take) every single day.

Remember, Martha Beck says it best, "How you do anything is how you do everything."

Here's to feeding that wolf on your left shoulder.

Chapter 12

You Weren't Born to Ask Permission

The only permission, the only validation, and the only
opinion that matters in our quest for greatness is our own.
—Dr. Steve Maraboli

Most people live "in between." They are not quite happy or sad. But are just comfortable enough to never do much about living the way they do. Over time, this will make you a follower.

To get out of this rut, we have to knock down the tower of mediocrity and start from the beginning if we aim to have a life of abundance and meaning.

You know, I don't remember anyone ever telling me that they asked to be born.

I can't recall anyone honestly ever blaming a baby for requiring too much attention. Every parent instinctively knows that when they bring a child into this world, it's their job to protect and provide.

So, how along the way did we learn to shrink to the opinion of others?

Never Play Small Again

Where in our journey did we stop dreaming and striving for everything we want in life?

Somewhere along the way, our authorities and experiences began to massage us into playing life smaller to avoid pain.

When this happens, we start seeking pleasure in the moment in the form of drugs, sex, and/or money. We trade our legacy for trinkets that sparkle but are worthless over time. That's because we aren't fulfilled.

When you become unfulfilled, you have two options:

1. Live in mediocrity and shrink your vision of who you are and your purpose.

2. Decide to break your chains of bondage, dare to dream, and begin to make powerful moves.

You weren't put on this planet to ask for permission to be you.

You don't owe anyone ANYTHING other than who you've given your word to. If you chose to make a promise, it's yours to keep. That's called integrity.

There are no subtle manipulative innuendos that hold you hostage other than what you're willing to tolerate, including the lies that temporary pleasure offers.

I see way too many people who've made silent agreements with others to remain small, lazy, and comfortable.

Success IS NOT found in your comfort zone.

The BEST Leaders ARE NOT just the ones calling the shots. They're the ones taking the shots ... and the arrows. The best leaders are those who are "in the trenches," doing their work to grow themselves.

This keeps them relevant, and it allows them to keep a finger on the pulse of those they lead. This is called leading from the front instead of the rear.

These leaders are the most inspiring and the most relatable. They become a living example for those who follow, to emulate in real-time for solutions to "now" problems.

Somehow, we're under the delusion that things will change for the better no matter what we do; that we just have to keep a positive attitude.

That's absolute HORSESHIT!

Things will begin to change when YOU change.

Your life will begin to change when you realize that you never have to ask permission to be 100% who you are. You were born with your gifts latent inside you, ready to burst from the seams.

All you have to do is remember where that spark is and commit to holding onto it. People and circumstances will try to make you conform, to try and force you to ask if it's okay for you to be you. You can and MUST stand against that resistance if you're going to fan a small flame into a raging fire.

Accomplishing small steps toward any goal is how you win; just make sure that what you set out to accomplish is in alignment with the life you believe you deserve.

On the other hand, you can set small goals to feel accomplished and build your self-image, but the reality is that YOU WILL KNOW you're capable of more.

You can lie all day to yourself and believe that you're getting better, but your subconscious mind knows you aren't really doing the work you're meant to do ... and it will haunt you.

Where the Rubber Meets the Road

Look in the mirror if you want to see the "in-between."

Look in your lover's eyes when you're intimate if you want to see the "in-between."

That "in-between" is where raw, naked vulnerability awaits you and forces you to notice all the shit you avoid because it scares the hell out of you.

In between what you think you know about yourself and what you REALLY believe is the REAL truth.

The in-between knows whether you'd really take a bullet for your friend or if all you'd do is pay lip service, thinking that day won't come.

MOST people in the world aren't here to make an impact.

MOST people in the world are quietly waiting to die; they avoid that inevitable truth by keeping their minds busy with things that have ZERO impact on their lives or those around them.

Like a dog who doesn't want to come home or a child who pretends she doesn't hear you when you call, avoiding the pain of death is one of the number one reasons people don't choose to discipline their minds.

Sure, people say the right words to appear that they're in control, but these words are often empty because the subconscious mind is programmed to be selfish. It's programmed to avoid death. I know because I used to be someone who loved people on the one hand and took from them on the other.

The root cause of this lack of integrity is most certainly selfishness and fear of loss. Facing your fears head-on is how you take the sting from the enemy.

Look, 99% isn't going to cut it either...

If you want a life of SIGNIFICANCE, a life worth remembering, and if you want to leave a LEGACY ...

If you don't want to DIE ALONE ...

If you DO want to have an IMPACT ...

Consider who you allow to feed your mind and who you allow into your inner circle.

Invest time with people who make no excuses for where they came from, where they are now, or where they're going. If you don't have these people in your life, you'd be better served alone with books, podcasts, and a pen and paper than with people who aren't willing to support YOUR "outlandish" goals.

Remember, you weren't born to ask for permission.

You were born to show the world WHO YOU REALLY ARE!

Chapter 13

You Can Be Right, or You Can Win

Discussions are always better than arguments,
because an argument is to find out who is right,
and a discussion is to find what is right.
—Unknown

How many damn times have I been in a situation where the person I'm talking to is misinformed ... AND talking *at* me instead of to me?

How many times have I blown my lid and said EXACTLY the wrong thing that left me with no way to recover?

I reflect on these questions because life seems to throw opportunities to people who have money, power, and "strategery" who keep their mouths shut and their eyes on the prize.

For so long, especially when I felt insignificant, I thought it was more important to win an individual argument instead of accomplishing my goals. I wonder if you can relate.

Over time, I've come to see a pattern, and I want to share it with you so that you might learn something that helps you close more "sales."

Being Right

When I was 20 years old, I dated a girl who was a little headstrong. We'd gone through the wringer for a couple of years, but I had decided that I was a committed dude and was in it for the long haul.

One day, her family invited me to go bowling. I was ecstatic to go because throwing "heavy balls at shit" was my jam.

Her mom, sisters, and even her uncles were there. Everyone was having a good time, but she had a lil' competition going on. It was the third round of bowling, and we were in the eighth frame. She and I were playing a single game and were tied, and it was her turn to bowl. As she bowled, one of her uncles came up to me and said: "Let her win. It'll be better for you."

So, I did.

On my next roll, I gently rolled it toward the gutter. She clapped and laughed.

I took a quick breath then rolled the second ball to hit two pins on the end. Again, she applauded.

She was next up and rolled her ninth shots. After that, I stepped up and rolled two gutter balls in a row.

She turned to me with a big grin and said, "You're doing that on purpose!"

I shrugged. "No, I'm not."

She rolled her tenth frame, and I came in last.

When the game was over, she ran up to me the moment I finished and immediately began to gloat.

I'm telling you ... it was the hardest thing NOT to say to her that I could have done better. It was such a pain to listen to her tell everyone that she kicked my ass ....

Yet, until I wrote this story down, I hadn't even considered that her uncles were watching me. It didn't dawn on me that I lived in a world LARGER than my own feelings and perceptions.

I wondered what these men thought about me, if they could relate, and if they chose to believe that I COULD do what's right, even when it's the hardest thing to do.

I wonder if they represent people in my life today, observing over time and choosing to believe what kind of person I truly am.

Living a life of principles DOES shape the quality of your life … and others are watching to see if you are who you say you are.

Let that shit sink in …

So, Here's The Real Question

Is it more relevant to you to be right or to accomplish your goals?

I watch salespeople all the time, talking about how the customer was an idiot or confrontational. I hear stories from people sharing their version of heartache on social media without context.

I wonder, *but did you get what you wanted?*

What are you hoping to accomplish by telling me how you were wronged?

Can you cash in the sympathy you get in your comments at the bank?

Can you use it to somehow insulate it from happening again by telling your woes?

Do you really feel better after spewing it online?

No … no … you're just telling me you don't know how to let it go and that if you don't win, it's "their" fault.

I don't know about you … but being right isn't nearly as satisfying as getting the results I want. Don't get me wrong, having someone misunderstand and malign you stings like a bitch, but I've learned that I can be right and lose the fight ... or I can let them say whatever suits them and win the day. I've come to learn that she or he who is the MOST intentional and sticks to their game plan the best almost always wins.

As you develop an inner circle of like-minded people, you might find more freedom in speaking how you feel, especially if those people are in pursuit of similar goals as you. Like many things, there is no hard and fast rule, but if I had to bet the farm on a particular result, I'd go with this:

Lead from the front, and let people win the battles while you focus on the war ...

Chapter 14

Busier than Hell and Still Not Winning?

It's not enough to be busy, so are ants.
The question is, what are we busy about?
—Henry David Thoreau

Allow me to tell you the story of how I learned the difference between being effective and being busy.

Before we get going, you need to understand that I'm the kind of guy who'd rather earn 1% of 100 people's efforts than 100% of one person's actions.

It is this focus that has allowed me to scale my income and reduce my workload.

The Art of Busy-ness

As I grew and scaled my business, it became more complex. I had to follow more rules, pay more taxes, put more systems in place, and sell more jobs; it went on and on and on.

One day, it dawned on me that the only job we were actually getting paid to do was taking the paintbrush and putting paint on the wall. The more color we took from the bucket and put on the wall, the faster we were paid.

Now, over the last 15 or 20 years, I've become more adept at what it means to take "paint from the bucket and put it on the wall." I've learned that highly successful people are still busy, but WHAT they choose to be engaged in is much different from the average person.

Highly focused individuals don't allow distractions, and they don't let needless conversations take place. They don't repeat themselves often and don't end up allowing other people to waste their time.

When I joined Apex Executives, founded by Ryan Stewman from Break Free Academy, it made me consider where I was in life. For the first time in my life, I had found a group of people at the top of their respective games, earning seven, eight, and even ten figures.

What really made me stop and consider my position wasn't the money, though. These men and women focus on success spherically and holistically. From their faith, fitness, finances, and family, every area is given the same focus: excellence.

For the first time, I could see that WHO I compared my success to was far too small.

What's even weirder is that I never knew I was comparing myself to others anyway. It was only when I could see others who were more successful AND younger than me that I realized my goals might need to be analyzed again.

This, in turn, reanimated dreams that I felt the door was slowly closing on. It gave me hope that maybe I could dream BIGGER again, and maybe I wouldn't live a life of quiet desperation anymore.

As I analyzed the MACRO evolutions and focused on my new "friends," my internal conversations helped me focus on the micro-decisions I made each day.

I thought about where I was allowing conversations to go on for three hours that were supposed to be 30 minutes.

I considered where I allowed other people's drama to take over my entire schedule.

I tried to recall how I allowed other people to exert control over me AND hold me accountable for my integrity while they obviously didn't apply the same level of scrutiny to themselves.

I started to learn that my "group" didn't think like me, have goals like me, nor were they willing to do what it really takes to be a champion in their own lives.

I was unequally yoked to people who loved to see me get on a pedestal, just so they could make themselves feel better when they threw tomatoes at me. I saw that I was sabotaging any real chance I had to live a life of significance as long as I invested my efforts into people who didn't truly have similar values as I do.

In studying very successful people, I observed they have a schedule they stick to.

Most people are extremely busy, but they still don't get what they want.

Success Differentiator

Successful people take the time to think about what they really want.

I've made it a habit of investing time into thinking about what I actually want in life and where I want to go.

Doing this has become a barometer for every decision that I make throughout the day.

I've found that the real answers come to me when I don't think I have anything left to think ... but I persist anyway. I commit my thoughts to paper. It's a good way to stay focused, especially when my mind struggles with that.

Pouring over my choices and why I do what I do, changes the dynamic of how I interact with my day and who I'm willing to have a conversation with. It lets me know how long I'm willing to have a conversation and for what purpose.

It's important to let people tell you what they think, but there comes a point when people tell you all about the labor but don't disclose much about "the birth." I don't have time to spend nine months with you exploring each day of that labor. Instead, let's talk about what happened once the baby came.

These questions keep me on track so I can optimize my time:

- What can I do to serve you?

- How can I help you?

- How is this information relevant, and why are you telling me this story?

I imagine you have goals you're trying to accomplish in life.

These are important aims for you. I have similar goals that I am striving to hit.

Yet, we allow other people to dominate our time and dictate to us what our day looks like. In essence, we end up not being in control of anything. When we act this way and respond this way, we allow other people to control everything except the one element that's MOST important: our responsibilities and commitments.

As a consumer or employer, you make promises to pay people money, and on the lowest level, you are responsible for making that happen. If money isn't the commitment, you've made promises of equal value, nonetheless.

When we let people dictate our time, we can't keep our word. Then we throw our hands up and tell the people we owe "money" to that we can't pay them. Of course, the people who have dictated our time aren't blamed for the inability to keep promises ... we are.

That's not too far off the mark because it's not the people who are wasting your time who are out of integrity; it's you.

When you have a dream that is so big and so far outside of what you know how to do, it becomes all-consuming to figure out how to accomplish it.

To understand what it takes to get what you want, you have to invest time away from the distractions and lean on a power greater than you.

If you don't do this, you might feel like a victim — as if there is nothing you can do and as if you didn't bring on these "uncontrollable" circumstances.

You Aren't a Victim Unless You Label Yourself That Way

Many of us fall into victim mode because events happen, sparking results that hold us back from what we desire.

We end up blaming a situation outside of ourselves, and that takes all of our power away to control it. If we would focus our time on what we truly want in personal and business matters, we'd look for ways to make that happen. Our focus would change, and eventually, we would stop blaming ourselves.

It's all about you ... Whatever you need to succeed is inside you. Yet, you give your personal power away to everyone else. Then, out of desperation, you start buying whatever silver bullet somebody is willing to offer, only to get angry at them because it didn't get you the result you wanted.

You literally start looking for quick fixes and shortcuts because you become more desperate for a result. Like a junkie, you eventually get hooked on whatever short-term pleasure you can get because your need for validation, your need for feeling something, is more important than anything else. This anxiety you feel kicks your fight or flight response into high gear, and it's no longer YOU who is running the show.

Sure, it feels like you (your conscious mind) are making decisions, but the truth is you are reacting to life instead of responding. You CAN stop the insanity, and it begins with this:

You have all the power you need in this world to accomplish everything that you want to achieve.

The problem is that most of us don't know what we want.

If you don't know what you want, how on earth can you ask somebody else to help you get it? On top of that, how will you know what conversations to have or what actions to take to get you there?

Spend some time genuinely thinking about what it is you want in life. Then you will have more control and less likelihood of feeling victimized.

I know I KEEP repeating this, and it's because, through repetition, you'll adopt this philosophy...

Being "Busy" is Overrated

This is your life. This is the chance that you have to receive it and experience it. This is your chance to produce the most beautiful painting EVER because nobody else will do it for you.

You, being busy, isn't very impressive to me.

You being effective and efficient is.

Making a mistake doesn't bother me.

Continuing to make the same mistake over and over again does.

I'm not going to invest my time with people who have to learn their lesson 18,000 different ways to get the first result. Not because I don't love people, not because I don't want you to get the result. Because you're not committed yet to what it is you want.

So, the next time you find yourself being "busy," ask yourself a simple question.

"How's being busy making me feel?"

Is being busy making you feel afraid?

Is being busy making you feel in your gut that you're just not getting "it" done?

Is being busy making you feel like you're spiraling out of control or that you're just not getting there?

If that's the case, then all you have to do is a simple exercise.

Do This to Get Back on Track

Stop, take a few deep breaths, and focus on what it is you want to accomplish.

From there, create an elementary list called: "I need to do this today." After you've completed your list, I suggest doing the most challenging task first and getting it out of the way.

As your energy wanes for the rest of the day, you can focus on more manageable and comfortable chores. When you accomplish those A's and B's, you'll find that the C's and D's might never come up. Still, you'll be moving closer and closer to your goal all the time.

We're all gonna die... The question is, are we ever really going to live? Are you strong enough to give up the thoughtless dogma of being busy and focus on being effective?

Are you ever really going to have a life of your design? It's truly a simple choice and one that only you can make.

Remember, the only person who can give you THAT freedom is you.

To learn additional ways you can kick "busy-ness" in the ass, sign up to work with me a www.kriswhitehead.com.

Chapter 15

Climbing the Summit of Success

Your success is determined by your ability to find solutions.
—Unknown

Most people make shit too complicated. I know because I'm always in between conversations with world-class successful people and those tangled in a knot, struggling to find their slice of the pie.

I am currently the director of coaches for Apex Executives. We help successful entrepreneurs become ELITE. I didn't start here, though.

I first began coaching in 1998 with my first four employees in a small remodeling business. By 2011, I had transitioned all my years of coaching to the professional world.

As I began Think to Succeed LLC, the idea was to help other business professionals learn about sales, marketing, and mindset. Social media was just getting its legs, and I thought it was a perfect platform to let the world know how I can help.

Boy, did it ever work. After millions in sales and clients from the four corners of the world, I learned two distinct characteristics about human nature.

1. People will do just about ANYTHING to avoid pain.

I don't care WHO you are. When given a choice to go through a fire or walk away, people will almost always choose to walk away or ignore the "elephant in the room."

It reminds me of the time I was coaching a medical team in Virginia.

It was a sunny Saturday in mid-March, and I'd just been picked up from the airport and shuttled to the function.

As people started to make their way in, everyone seemed to be buzzing with energy and excitement.

I made it a point to greet everyone and find out at least one fact about them that was unique and what they hoped the day would accomplish.

Everything was going smoothly until I met one of the vendor reps who was only there to "see what his money bought him."

At $5,000 per day, I could understand … and I promise I wasn't there to disappoint.

Our first activity called for everyone to stand in a circle. Imagine 35 people in a giant room forming a circle about 40 feet in diameter.

When everyone quieted down, I pulled out a ball of duct tape from my pocket, then immediately grabbed another roll of tape after tossing the first one to someone across the room. I snarled up the duct tape from that first roll into a big ball. Then worked on the next roll and so on.

People made jokes and murmured as I stood there wadding up the tape. I was with doctors, techs, and admins, throwing balls of duct tape to them without saying a word.

After I'd made four balls, I told them the rules:

- You will be timed.

- All four balls must pass through everyone's hands.

- You cannot pass a ball to the person beside you.

We went through one practice run with me leading the pack. I then pulled myself from the pack, repeated the instructions above, and said, "I'll time you now. Any last questions?" No matter what anyone asked, I just repeated the three rules above.

When I said go, it was complete pandemonium. Loud talking, balls flying everywhere. The group completed the game in one minute and 30 seconds.

I turned to them and asked, "Is that the best you got?"

Of course, the answer was a loud, "NO!"

They kept refining their process until they'd gotten it down to about 55 seconds. I could see the different reactions on people's faces and read their body language.

There was the Alpha: *WE WILL WIN.*

The beta: *THIS IS STUPID.*

And the DELTA" *Kris is stupid.* Lol…

So, I let them know that the last team of the same size I'd timed had gotten it down to 15 seconds.

After the jeers, name-calling, and arguing, the "leaders" emerged. What was surprising was that it wasn't the doctors or managers.

There was a guy who cleaned up the messes in the operating rooms who calmly waited for everyone to quiet down before he spoke.

With simple instructions and relative ease, he described a scenario where all the rules could be followed AND time reduced.

Everyone allowed him to be the leader and show them what he meant.

Everyone EXCEPT the rep whose company had paid for the event. He quite literally was in the corner pouting. This was exactly what the game was designed to elicit from people.

By taking people's minds off THEMSELVES, their true nature would be revealed. Winners who never spoke up for themselves were forced to because no one else had an answer.

Losers, who posed as winners, also showed themselves because they weren't "team" players. If they couldn't win alone, they couldn't take the time to listen to others "beneath" them.

That day, I learned to SEE people's actions and let them teach me who they are, not just their words. Leaders can be the most unlikely of heroes when given the chance to shine.

2. People will buy AND expect YOU to do their work.

Coaching others can be tricky business. The untold secret is that you, as a coach, attract clients who are just like you.

If you're trying to help people find success, you better make damn sure you've gotten it for yourself first.

When I first began selling marketing and software online, I found it pretty easy to get people to pay me money for services.

What wasn't easy was for them to remember what they'd bought!

Even three months later, clients would be confused and not remember why we were working together.

This is where I learned about integrity.

It's easy to promote yourself as a badass on social media. It's also easy to sell to people who are desperate for results.

The problem comes in when the client doesn't have a clear idea of the results they want.

Clients only become these kinds of clients because YOU or I allow them to be.

The lesson I learned is that I need to know EXACTLY how I help people. EXACTLY what kind of results I offer and what the client's role is in achieving said results.

If you don't want to sell to desperate people … don't be desperate.

It doesn't matter whether someone is wealthy or poor. Desperate people cling to other desperate souls.

Elevate yourself to being exceptional at what you do, and you will find those who want those results, too. I promise, with over eight billion people in the world and the ease of communication today, you can win if you know who you are and what you do.

The Three Factors of Success

After years of observation, implementation, and coaching other business owners, I can tell you that ANY of the success you want to achieve boils down to three factors.

1. You have to get super clear on what it is you really want.

Too many people in the world follow after SOMEONE else's dream. It isn't because they're stupid; it's because they're lazy. Lazy people attach to someone else's dream because they haven't taken the time to ask themselves who they really are, what truly makes them feel fulfilled, and why they believe their life is significant.

The problem is that NONE of us are willing to "go all-in" 100% for someone else. It just isn't sustainable. You can't be someone else's everything because you'll have nothing left for yourself. Their dream is theirs … and you cannot commit to someone else if you cannot first FULLY commit to yourself. Even if you're just 1% away from going all in, it isn't enough when the shit hits the fan. The pain is too great a burden to bear to maintain a vision that isn't yours. It also isn't playing the odds in life because we're preprogrammed to be selfish out of basic survival.

Why fight that instinct?

Instead, use it to your advantage to find what you're really willing to commit to with everything you've got.

We've got a saying around our offices, "You'll know how much you believe in something the moment you choose to quit."

When you are willing to do the work and find what you really want, you'll subconsciously make a decision to go over, under, or through whatever it takes to achieve it.

2. Recognize your self-talk.

I promise you that world-class people don't allow defeatist conversations to ingrain themselves in their heads.

But refusing that self-talk requires training. You either need to have a long streak of wins to lean on and remind yourself of during the tough times, or you need to fill your mind with positive affirmations BEFORE tough times come.

Mental motivators act as reserve fuel when you need it most, so you aren't stopped dead in your tracks when life rings your bell. If you aren't doing the work you need to do during peacetime, I promise you'll bleed during wartime.

Learning how to be your own "hype-man" is the only way to guarantee that you will hear the right message when you need it most.

There's no safety net for those who are climbing to the summit of success. Act like your life depends on it because it does.

3. Find a "family" where you BELONG.

Since our species is community-based, we will ALL find a family or group. This is rooted in basic survival.

If you are not using this instinct to your advantage, why not?

Most people don't ever consider that they have a choice to stay, change, or go it alone. The truth is you do. No one is forcing you to stay with people who aren't working for the same life experiences you are. No one is keeping you chained to your family of origin. No one is forcing you to stay with your spouse, your parents, or your friends who are continuously derailing you from focusing on being the best version of yourself.

People stay in groups that don't serve them usually because they don't know what they really want. They allow the conversations of their group to resonate louder in their head than their self-talk.

This is where that "knot" of confusion usually begins. It creates a cluttered mind that, that by default, usually does nothing. You can't take the loss and move forward because you were sabotaged before you ever began.

The right group will be those who are in search of the same objectives you are. They're willing to stretch and reach for what they really want. They'll represent the "can do" attitude and an unwavering determination to do whatever it takes to succeed.

They'll do the work, regardless of the short-term results, because they are 100% locked into the idea that they MUST have what they want. There is NO PRICE too large to pay for the outcome because there is NO PURPOSE higher than the one they've gotten clear on — the one they want to achieve most in their life.

Lastly, to achieve the summit of success, there is only one more thing you MUST do.

NEVER ... never, never quit.

I don't know exactly how or when you will achieve your goals, but that isn't the point of life anyway. All the greats know that, too.

The point is the journey. Confidence, joy, and the beauty of life come from someone on a larger mission that involves more than themselves. Find something other than ONLY what supports you. Giving back, nurturing, and growing the next round of leaders is how we move society forward.

Champions may be initially drawn in by the spoils of their labor. But eventually, they come to realize it's the journey that's so damn meaningful.

My teams and I live by the saying, "You're either growing, or you're dying." I sure hope you choose to live the same way.

Throughout life, you'll meet some cool people, become the hero in your own story, and find purpose in your struggle.

You'll come to find that the summit of success is never a destination. It's only a place to plant your flag for others to use as a beacon and for you to stand on to see further and dream bigger.

Chapter 16

If Not Now...When?

Each moment is a place you've never been.
—Mark Strand

Challenge me if I'm wrong, but most of the failures we experience in life aren't due to our lack of preparedness. They don't come down to a tactical strategy we didn't know about or anything situational. Most of us fail because we didn't really want what we thought we wanted. Whether we're talking about your job, your business, or your marriage, you fail when you stop. Until you've called it quits on something; you haven't failed ... you've only found one way that something doesn't work.

So, why is it that we spend so much time experiencing a life that leads to failure instead of deliberately planning one that leads to success?

Many of us spend our lives doing so much for others that we cheat ourselves. From a young age, we are taught that our hopes and dreams aren't as important as those dreams of others around us. Our parents didn't know how to treat each other right, so they certainly didn't know how to show us what it looks like to love, encourage, and nurture balanced relationships.

We learned that we could be the selfish asshat or the one who gives everything and asks for nothing in return. Of course, there are many variations between these extremes!

As we grow up, we give to our spouse, our kids, and our customers hoping they will love us for our efforts, when often they just expect something different than what we're offering. We often use their unfulfilled needs as fuel to justify a life of martyrdom that keeps us weak and powerless. When you are in this state, it can make you look like a meek, mild-tempered, and passive-aggressive person ... or it can make you rage like a chest-pounding asshole when you decide you've tolerated enough.

I'm not here to psychoanalyze you, and I suggest you don't waste any time trying to do that to yourself or anyone else either. Not that it isn't helpful, but I'm not qualified, and quite frankly, you probably aren't either. Instead, why not take the time to do what simply works and get busy doing the ONE thing that will get you firmly placed on the long journey of a life well-lived?

What is that ONE thing? What comes to mind?

If you only had one more thing you could accomplish before you died, what would it be? Assume that you'll be given exactly the right amount of time to get it done.

If you had to choose that ONE thing ... what would you choose?

Figure it out and commit to it.

Perspective Exercise

Let's do a quick exercise so you can gain a little perspective. Find a tape measure and pull the tape out until you find 78 inches. Lock the measure, so the tape stays out, set it on the ground, and look at the numbers. Count up until you find the number that correlates with your age. I'd be on 46" because I'm 46 years old. When you find your number, see how far away it is from seventy-eight.

If the average life expectancy of a man in the Western world is 78 years, I'm more than halfway to that number by the tape measure.

Where do you fall on the tape measure?

Regardless of where you are, you won't have any more tape to play with at some point. So, what is it that you really want to do with the time you have left?

Think Time

One of the most powerful exercises I've invested in early in the morning is "think time." During this time, I work on my <G>code, created by my friend Ryan Stewman. My <G> is what I'm grateful for, my wins yesterday, accountability for my fitness, and what lessons I learned. I also take it a step further and ask myself, what I really want is?

Then I focus on getting clear about what an ideal life looks like for me. I don't worry about how I'm going to do it; I don't worry about how silly it sounds, and I don't focus on anyone else's feelings or wants.

This is MY time to talk to God and make a list like he's Santa Claus.

The funny thing is it may start with stuff ... but the more time you invest in the exercise, the more you'll uncover what really fires you up. You'll find what you're willing to relentlessly pursue regardless of the roadblocks that present themselves.

As I said earlier, most people in life don't have what they want because they *don't know* what they want.

Here's a simple and effective strategy to find what you really want ...

And please note, I promise when you know what you want, the "how" will show up. It will show up because your mind will be predisposed to create solutions. If you are slack on giving your mind precise input, it'll go to work with the haphazard information it receives. When you focus on what you want, get crystal clear on what you want, and tell your mind

EXACTLY what you want, your subconscious will go to work in the background, helping you become aware of the opportunities to make your thoughts a reality.

All this strategy requires is 20 minutes of uninterrupted time with a sheet of paper and a pen. You'll simply write, "What I want is..." until you're out of ideas.

Then, commit to continue to write once you hit THE WALL. You'll know you've hit the wall when you start to get fidgety. When you draw a blank, and a cold bead of sweat drips down your forehead. You'll know you're at THE WALL when you start feeling the urge to stop.

This is a powerful way to uncover what really drives you forward.

So, the question really is, if not now ... when?

You've been beating your head against a wall forever, wondering WHY?

Why can't I stick to a plan?

Why do I feel unfulfilled?

Why am I so confused?

Why am I eating, drinking, and/or smoking too much?

Why?

Why not ask yourself a really amazing question instead?

What do I really want?

When you get clear on what you want, you'll get supercharged on finding creative ways to get it. It'll also make you the hero in your own story, with your own adventures. Instead of watching someone else's highlight reel on social media, you'll create one of your own!

Chapter 17

There is No Plan B

The strongest factor for success is self-esteem. Believing you can do it, believing you deserve it and believing you'll get it.
—Unknown

How many people who have experienced EPIC success have told you they got "lucky"?

I don't mean they had a good month or even a good year. I'm talking about long-term, sustainable, and growing success.

The problem for most is, we see someone who's already successful, making moves and "easily" crushing it. Then it becomes easy to start thinking, *if I had what they have, I'd be successful, too.* You may be right, but I'd bet you'd have a tough time keeping and growing that success.

What's given can so quickly be taken, but the wisdom that you earn can be applied to just about any area of your life for as long as you're alive. Most people's trouble is that they're always looking for the shortcut, the loophole, or the NEW fad diet.

It's tough to gain wisdom with shortcuts, and it becomes increasingly challenging to know how to steer your ship in rough waters when you didn't take the time to practice when it was calmer.

After years of coaching other business owners and looking for similarities among those who have long-term success, I've found several constants to attaining success among them all.

Once I compiled that list, I dove deeper to look for the #1 reason or similarity that must be present to have success.

There were some significant contenders for the #1 spot, from setting big goals and having a healthy self-image to the ability to delegate and networking with the right people. So many people I know are working on one or all of these, and they still struggle, so there had to be a master key. There had to be one secret, that once unlocked, would virtually guarantee that someone would accomplish what they set out to do.

An Unlikely Hero

One day, as I was wrestling with what it could be, I heard a headline story of a young girl who was trapped under an overturned car. I'll never forget how the reporter described the vehicle beginning to catch fire and how the police were dumbfounded when they arrived at the scene.

After someone called 911, the mother of the young girl was frantic as she saw the flames engulf the car. She was afraid no one would show up in time to rescue her daughter before she was burned alive, so she sprang into action. When the authorities showed up, the mom and her child were sitting on the roadside about 100 yards away from the charred wreckage.

When the police asked the mother how her daughter had gotten out from under the burning car, she simply said, "I lifted the car up enough for her to get out." She had lifted a vehicle over 4000 lbs. high enough in the air for her daughter to escape.

I remember as I listened to her act of bravery, the pain she'd had to endure: burned hands, no help, and impending doom. I also remember being smacked in the head with the most OBVIOUS answer to achieving ALL kinds of success.

When you don't give yourself any other option than success, you'll get it. Just like that mama with her baby trapped under a burning car, you have to be so determined about the goal that YOU WILL CHOOSE to do what MUST BE DONE to get it.

When you leave yourself an escape, you'll most likely take it when the going gets tough. You MUST CHOOSE that there is no plan B. No matter how grim it looks, no matter who comes against you, no matter what ...

This is THE singular defining quality amongst the highest achieving and most successful people I've ever witnessed to achieve the results that everyone else wonders at. Winners give themselves ONLY one option. Succeed ... or die trying.

There is no price too high, no rock they won't overturn, no action too silly to do.

In a breakfast of eggs and bacon, the chicken is involved ... but the pig, he's committed.

My question to you is:

Are you REALLY committed to getting what you want?

Chapter 18

How Are You Showing Up?

Can you remember who you were before the world told you who you should be? -Charles Bukowski

One of the most significant business and life lessons I learned was the benefit of showing up when it counts most.

Sadly, we, as consumers, have come to expect mediocrity from the services and products we purchase. Excellent service after the sale is the exception, not the rule. Maybe it's because, as consumers, we know deep down that we are only willing to go so far to honor our own commitments. We tolerate in others what we justify in our own behavior. We make excuses for others who malign us because we can relate. This isn't a recipe for value ... it's a slow death march because today's exceptions become tomorrow's rules.

I want to share a couple of personal stories with you that might help you reconsider how much your integrity is worth.

Story #1

Yesterday, I was having a conversation with one of my sales guys. He makes around $350,000/year and loves to barter. When one of our home-owners is getting rid of a stove, he'll take it. Windows, doors, you name it, if it's in good shape, he's on the prowl to get things for free and turn around and sell them.

So, I asked him yesterday, "You really like to barter, don't you?"

He said, "If it's a great deal for them and a pretty good deal for me, I'm all for it." He then immediately followed up with, "If it's a great deal for me and an okay deal for them, that's what I'm about."

I did a double-take and kept my mouth shut.

But what I was thinking was, which is it, man?

After reflecting on it for a while, I decided his REAL truth was in his second sentence.

> **In his mind, he's convinced himself that he's a good guy who's taking care of others first, but his truth is he's still a self-serving puke.**

This leads me to think about how I used to show up and when I learned where the truth always comes out. About 20 years ago, I was a subcontractor running a painting crew that worked for high-end construction companies. I'll never forget the day I interviewed with a new production manager and told him with energy and vehemence that he could count on me. When the going got tough, we'd be there, no matter what.

About a month later, some of my guys dripped paint all over a new roof. It was three stories high, and I guess they thought no one would see, so they didn't say anything to me. But the production manager saw it and called me. I said something about it being out of eyesight. He immediately snapped back, "Remember when you said you'd be there no matter what? Now's the time to prove it."

So, we did. My guys went up there and covered the yellow paint with black spray paint.

The PM called me the next day, livid! I had to fix the situation. To get rid of the black spray paint, we had to pay a roofing company to remove and replace the shingles, and we lost any future work with them.

To say I learned a valuable lesson is an understatement.

Getting caught being half-ass is not only embarrassing; it immediately classified me in my own mind as a poor bum of a contractor.

I want you to learn from my mistake, so you don't have to feel pain from making your own.

It took me years of playing second fiddle, developing my self-image, and choosing to believe that I can create a company (people of substance) worth what we charge, market uniquely and profitably, and produce amazing results for our clients consistently.

It was during these painful, financially unprofitable years that I learned what my integrity was worth. Selling is easy. It isn't hard to tell people what they want to hear. And it's easy to get people caught up in an emotional buying frenzy, collect their money, and push them down the line for others to fulfill the request. It's also easy to forget the promises you make after you've gotten what you wanted.

Be different.

Live in integrity and remember that your customers are looking for a result, not your product or service.

They don't care about why things don't work out, only about making sure they get what they want.

Take the time to understand their expectations EXACTLY and make sure you can deliver MORE than what you tell them. It's a simple recipe for long-term success.

Make a decision today to pay the full price for integrity. You'll find that when you slip, you'll be in a stronger position to recover the sale, the client's loyalty and create repeat or referral business.

Chapter 19

Running the Red Line

He that is good for making excuses
is seldom good for anything else.
—*Benjamin Franklin*

So many people are Running the Red Line of life. The problem is, we don't have a tachometer, like a car, to tell us we're getting close to burning our engine out.

Most people are only one or two heartbreaks away from losing everything they have. Worse yet, they will spiral out of control if it happens.

The time for playing games is over.

There is a specific difference between those who have the mindset of a champion and everyone else who makes excuses for where they are in life. Champions don't get caught up in the game; they strive for the win!

With all the information on what success looks like, it's no wonder why so many struggle to find lasting success.

We have a little voice that calls out in the wee hours of the night.

It's that little voice that shows up when we're stressed, surprised, or a significant calamity hits us in the face that we weren't expecting. Most of the time, it's the ONLY OPPORTUNITY we have to know it's even there.

I like to call it our "Bitch Voice."

Even though most of us go along all day, every day with it playing in our heads, we barely pick up on it.

We have drama in our family, business, and friendships that can distract us.

We have social media, television, and doom-and-gloom messages hitting us everywhere we turn.

Most people are too mentally weak to resist the urges of drifting into becoming an unconscious follower.

The powers that "BE" have billions of dollars and years of experience in luring us to follow their direction and participate for the benefit of their cause.

Hell, I've watched grown-ass men get more emotional about the outcome of a football game than their own personal trajectory.

I've seen people who are more attached to their sister's drama, their best friend's life, or how many likes and comments they get on their social media status.

I've hung around people who are absolute ROCKSTARS at making money OR living a healthy lifestyle ... but rarely do I witness both.

Rarely do I witness a winner in their relationships, self-mastery, finances, and health. Can you really say you're winning unless you find success in all areas of your life?

I don't know about you,
but I'm an ambitiously lazy kinda guy.

I want to KNOW the foundational exercises I could deploy into my life so that at the end of it, I would know that I squeezed every bit of fun, success, and learning out of it that I wanted to.

I would know that I had lived a life without regret.

Quitters allow their bitch voice to win instead of their boss voice.

They make promises when they're motivated and forget those promises when "life" isn't as easy.

They make excuses as to why they can't do what they are working toward.

"I got fired."

"I'm sick."

"It's because of COVID-19."

Any excuse will do for the bitch voice to win.

But the boss voice only needs one reason to win.

"Because I said so."

This commitment and keeping your promise are called integrity. The best way to learn to live in it is to sweat in peacetime.

Sweating in peacetime refers to your ability to practice habits that will be second nature when you're stressed out. All of us would love to think we can save the day when something freaks us out. If you're trained, then yes, I'd bet on you all day long over someone who has no experience in that particular situation.

Why not build the consistent habits of success—the foundational habits you choose to live by—so that when you are scared, you react consistently and well?

When things are going easy, push yourself to that red line!

Prove to YOURSELF that you DO have what it takes, no matter what!

Teach your body to succumb to your mind.

Teach your mind to succumb to your will.

This is the mindset of a champion.

Sure, you might fail in the process, but who would you rather be — someone who is "in it" until the going gets tough, or someone you know you can count on NO MATTER the circumstances?

Your answer to that question is all you'll ever need to know in life. What you might find, like those of us who are always striving to become better, is that you WIN way more often than you lose.

That's because you have staying power while others who are weaker-minded will fall to the wayside.

There are NO trophies in life for living "second best." Get that shit out of your head and determine to become who you are truly meant to be:

A BOSS!

All it takes is one quality decision and the tenacity to stick to your guns.

Chapter 20

Becoming the Champion of Change

Every champion was once a contender that refused to give up.
—Rocky Balboa, Rocky

You want to be the baddest MF'r in the room, period.

You know it.

I know it.

Everyone is clambering to see who can outshine the other, say the wittiest thing, or have their ego stroked.

Every Alpha I know lives for that shit, so denying it will just keep you that much farther away from having it.

What is it about those people who walk into a room, and EVERYONE notices them? They just have a presence about them, don't they?

What is it that separates those who command respect versus those who try to force you to respect them?

That presence we all feel is the "smoke of battle" that's all over them.

That smoke is CERTAINTY.

Certainty has a way of giving someone an edge of confidence.

Certainty has a way of turning a chump into a champ.

> **Every champion knows that if they're going to bet on someone, it's themselves. They've gone through the fire, and they've been forged into a weapon.**

Everything that doesn't serve their cause is stripped away, either purposefully because it's a hindrance to their goals or coincidentally because the harder they work, the "luckier" they get.

A champion has created an endless feedback loop of action, desire, and faith.

Take a look at this simple graphic, inspired by Napoleon Hill in his world-renown book, *Think and Grow Rich*:

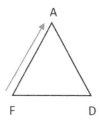

Before Faith, there is belief...
and that belief leads to action.

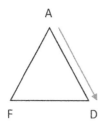

That Action leads to a budding desire.

That Desire leads to increased belief and finally Faith. Faith that Increases Action...which feeds the Desire... until the repeated Pattern builds to a WHITE HOT Desire for your intended outcome.

A champion has chosen over and over again to use this model to build an incredible self-image over time. They've learned to face any challenge in life and quickly take action as they overcome inevitable hurdles. Once clearing these hurdles, their desire for the reward increases.

While most people struggle and feel pain, champions fuel their faith with a burning desire that leads to increased action and seemingly less effort.

When they reach this point, their only requirement is to remember to continue to take action. Their self-doubt and all other forms of negative reinforcement have less and less ability to stop the repeated actions of failure from taking place. It is those refined and repeated actions that lead to their eventual successful outcome every single time.

It's a certainty.

Very few people have it, and those who do aren't lucky. They're just sure.

They're sure that what separates them from everyone else in the room is their willingness to make the changes required to fulfill their ability to be the most elite version of themselves.

Champions realize that leadership is simply changing and evolving faster than others.

They know they always have value to share because not many people are willing to take actions that lead to real change.

Your focus can become your superpower when you decide what you want and become willing to take action toward that goal.

Are you strong enough to be a champion of change?

Chapter 21

The Real Function of Fear

Don't be afraid of your fears. They're not there to scare you.
They're there to let you know that something is worth it.
—C. JoyBell C.

It's common sense to run away from what scares the shit out of you.

It's programmed into our DNA to either run away or fight when something is a perceived threat.

Truth be told, we're probably mostly descended from people who chose to go back and hide in the cave instead of the drunk guy running to piss on the sabretooth tiger just to see if it can be done. That said, fear is nothing to be ashamed of because you literally can't stop the response, no matter how seasoned a fighter you are.

There's also a big difference between surviving and thriving.

I believe with generations of programming teaching us to run away from our fears; it's uncommon to see people stand, face, and conquer them, too.

My good buddy's job is to punch his clients in the nose when they start working together.

He owns many martial arts studios, and the reason he punches them is that the initial response when you get punched in the nose (assuming it's never happened before) is to freeze.

His clients hire him to teach them to be victorious when fighting, and all it takes is a split-second of "WTF" for a fight to go south really quickly.

By punching his clients in the nose, he's giving them the experience to feel, learn, and override the natural response everyone has when processing new information.

There are also levels to this getting punched in the nose.

Just ask any one of Mike Tyson's victims who have been in the ring with him. You have to be ready for your opponent and have a strategy if you aim to win. Muhammad Ali chose a bold approach against a young George Foreman. This is where the term "rope-a-dope" came from. Ali went round after round with his back against the ropes, letting big ol' Foreman chop away at him like a giant redwood tree.

The fight didn't start in the ring, though. Ali was in Africa weeks before the Rumble in the Jungle began, taunting Foreman, getting into his head. In interviews and other promotional footage, Ali was using the media to speak directly to Mr. Foreman.

On the night of the fight, at the opening bell of the second round, 60,000 African fans started chanting, "Ali, boombayah," or "Ali, kill him." At that moment, Ali was looking for one thing, the dawning of doubt or fear in his opponent's eyes. In round eight, after Foreman's will to win began to flicker, Ali turned on the "sting" and put Foreman on his ass to win the match.

You can't tell me that Ali didn't feel fear. You can't tell me that my friend's clients, seeing the student next to them take a punch to the nose without flinching, don't feel the fear. The difference between them and everyone who freezes, recoils, or runs from fear is their ability to take it and keep moving forward. They can do it because they have a strategy in place for doing so.

If you're going to live a life you're proud of, you have to rise above your fears. You have to be willing to call your shots, take a few in return, and stick to the plan even when you're quaking in your boots.

You have to shut down your doubts and find reasons to keep on the path. You have to be so committed to your goal that you're willing to sacrifice your fears to achieve it. It's just how winning is done.

You have to understand that the only limit out there is the one you place on yourself...

THAT'S NOT YOU! You're better than that, and it's time to get what you're worth.

It's time to start using fear to your advantage as a barometer, to know you're taking on challenges worthy of your destiny.

It's time to stop looking for the easy way out.

It's time to stop flinching and freezing every time you're stunned by fear.

It's time to stop shrinking back into the cave because it's "safer" there.

We're all going to die. My question to you is ... DO YOU WANT TO LIVE?

If so, it's time to master your fears by facing them and knowing WHEN to go all in.

Chapter 22

"No" is a Complete Sentence

The art of leadership is saying no, not saying yes.
It is very easy to say yes.
—*Tony Blair*

Over the years, and after a metric shit-ton of personal development, I began to identify a pattern I saw in many salespeople and entrepreneurs. This pattern is so subtle that most people dismiss it under the guise of being "nice" or "reasonable."

It's one of the most disempowering habits that lead to failed dreams, playing small, and living a life of frustration. It diverts a would-be champion into a lame duck and neutralizes any chance of living a truly unique life filled with purpose.

Feeling guilty for what you believe isn't natural; it's learned. It's the main reason why people feel the need to explain themselves when they know they're getting ready to say something that another won't like.

Here's a story to help you see it more clearly.

Family Pressure

I was sitting at the dinner table with my daughter last week, and she was conflicted about going to visit her grandmother for the weekend. She was about two weeks away from her freshman year at college and sensed the transition point of full adulthood coming at her like a freight train.

As I sat and listened to her tell her mom that she didn't really want to go to her grandmother's house, I got lost in EVERYONE else's emotions that she was trying to untangle.

My daughter eventually came up with the idea that she could tell her grandmother a little white lie and excuse herself from the visit.

Until then, I had just chosen to observe, but now was the time to speak up:

"You don't have to lie. You can just say no," I told her.

Her dilemma about what to do made me think of my years growing up and all the years in business where I did the same thing. I had spent more time worrying about whether I was offending, upsetting, or disturbing others than I did about my own well-being. Doing that often led to business deals and even friendships that weren't really in my favor.

Usually, I would find myself on the short end of the relationship, or I wouldn't make enough money for the time I'd invested in jobs. Like my daughter wanted to, I'd eventually follow the path of least resistance and lie or fold and do things that weren't in my best interest.

Investing mental energy into people who aren't nearly as worried about a balanced relationship says a lot more about you than it does anyone else. If you take the time to follow that rabbit down the hole, you might find that you don't have as much respect for yourself as you could.

How can we expect others to respect us at a higher level than we do ourselves? We're all teaching everyone every day what we'll tolerate. The clearer you are about your self-respect, the more likely you are to hold the line when others treat you with less dignity than you deserve. Holding the line doesn't mean you harm someone in return, either. In fact, you'll most likely empower someone to see a broader perspective by standing in your truth.

How can we expect to attract any relationship worthy of our ideals when we don't live by them?

The problem for most of us is that we judge others by their actions and ourselves by our intentions. We resort to lying to others because we have first lied to ourselves.

Once when I was nine years old, I was at a sleepover and had poison ivy all over my arms. I told my buddy it itched, and he said, "Don't scratch it, just rub it." That sounded like good advice, so I did ... all damn night. By the next morning, my arm looked like a cooked hotdog. As I reflect back now, I can see that I took his advice because I wanted to scratch my arm one way or another. I believed the lie because it served my real intention.

The truth is you ARE getting everything in life you want right now. As hard as it might be to swallow, your thoughts have created your actions, and they have led you to your results. Learning to live in your truth comes with a cost, but it's cheaper than what you will pay to believe your lies.

Take the time to see how often people around you negotiate their integrity away, and you'll see the pattern too. The pattern of trying to please everyone. Most people's default mechanism is to give in to someone else at the expense of themselves. This leads to feeling less and less fulfilled, which leads to more disempowering habits.

Remember, "NO" is a complete sentence.

Although it may be uncomfortable to say at first, you'll see who respects you for you when you respect yourself enough to call it like you see it.

Chapter 23

Just Because You Bought It, Doesn't Mean You Own It

If you think it's expensive to hire a professional,
wait until you hire an amateur.
—Unknown

People continually let everyone know how disappointed they are in customer service.

Of course, this makes sense because they paid for a product or service and expect the result that was promised. In the same vein, I also see many business owners get pissed off when they purchase something, but the trouble often is that taking the time to complain doesn't get them to their overall goals.

So, what do you do to guarantee that you will GET what you pay for? I'll share a mindset shift that has helped my clients and me find better results. It begins with a story about a Wendy's drive-through.

The Drive-Through

Last week, Robyn and I were on our way to the airport and hadn't eaten all morning. Although we don't often eat fast food, we decided to hit up a local Wendy's drive-through for a quick meal before our flight.

As I rolled up to the speaker, a voice asked what we'd like, and I said, "A number one … ketchup, mustard, and pickles only."

After a brief pause, I said, "Medium (size) and a Diet Dr. Pepper."

Then realizing that number ones consist of a single, double, or triple patty now, I said, "Make that a single." Then I paused again, waiting for the familiar, "Is there anything else, or will that complete your order?"

Instead, the voice said, "A number one, single, with pickles and what else?" I repeated, "Ketchup, mustard, and pickles."

The lady asked, "And a Dr. Pepper?"

I said, "Diet."

"Okay, anything else?"

I said, "Another number one, double, medium, with an unsweetened iced tea."

At the pick-up window, the clerk handed me a tea. Before I grabbed it, I said, "Unsweetened?"

The clerk shook her head at me and said, "SWEETENED."

Honestly, she sounded a little like the Soup Nazi from Seinfeld. It was apparent that she hadn't heard my intention, and honestly, I didn't care anymore at that point.

As we drove down the road, it dawned on me how and why I hadn't gotten what I'd wanted in the way I thought I should have gotten it.

HERE'S WHERE A LOT OF FOLKS GET DERAILED AND LOSE THE OPPORTUNITY TO GET BETTER RESULTS.

I looked at my wife and said, "That was totally my fault. In fact, I just crystallized on a lesson that keeps so many people from getting what they want in life."

The rest of my learning lesson is below:

How many times do we give ourselves permission to be upset at others because we've consciously or subconsciously made an agreement with someone else then DIDN'T get what we expected?

A common misconception exists in the world that because you give money to someone, you immediately become the boss of that situation.

Okay, if you are going to be a boss, then I'm going to share with you what that really means.

Being a boss means YOU are 100% responsible for the results you get.

Have you ever had a boss demean you? Call you out, show you all the ways you've made a mistake, and then punish you by making you grovel, promise, or work even harder for less of a reward?

If so, how did it make you feel?

Sure, maybe you did what was required, but did it propel you toward more significant and more consistent achievements?

If not, then why do we blame the person trying to fulfill our requests without first taking stock to see if we gave the best instructions?

I gave that young lady at Wendy's horrible directions on the first order. I asked for the meals and the ingredients ALL OUT OF ORDER and didn't get what I asked for. Maybe if I had taken a little time and thought about the sequence and what I should have ordered, I could have gotten a better result.

I probably had her hitting buttons, thinking... is it a single burger or what while I was asking for a DIET Doctor Pepper. By the time I'd figured out my cadence and ordered the double, she was already struggling with mind-drifting. It's like when you say, "Take care" to someone after they've helped you and they say, "You're welcome." Mind drifting, unaware, blissfully ignorant...

From our prospects to our employees, we have a cadence and a rhythm we follow in communication. Often, we fail miserably to detect whether they are on our wavelength when we're speaking to them. We make assumptions, mistakes and aren't systematic in our process of delivering critical information at the right time to the person who's listening to us.

When they fail to deliver, it's easy to get mad and judge them for it. If you've been in business for any length of time with any measurable result, you've had a client treat you precisely this same way.

Sure, sometimes they might've had a right to be upset, especially if you are out of integrity with something you've promised.

What about when you were in integrity? Didn't you just wish they could see it a little bit from your perspective? Weren't you sure that they might just calm down if they did pause and reflect, and you could find a solution together? Because you knew that you'd be willing to do almost anything to make it right...

So, the next time you're not getting the results you want, and it's attached to someone else's efforts, pause before you tear apart their lack of integrity or process. Take the time to make sure that you are communicating clearly, in a way they can process.

If you're the boss, act like one and learn how to lead by showing others how to best follow. Often, learning their language and patterns of doing things is the best way to communicate to them.

Chapter 24

Who Will Do What by When?

The single biggest problem in communication
is the illusion that it has taken place.
—George Bernard Shaw

One of the TOP mistakes I have made in the past, and I often see others making, is not structuring and adhering to time management when communicating with others.

As I left the field to scale our business, I found it more challenging to communicate effectively with our men in the field when it came to deadlines.

It seemed that their idea of the pace of completing tasks was, "It'll get done when it's done," or "It is what it is."

That doesn't sit well for scheduling different trades on top of each other or back-to-back jobs. It pisses clients off when we're working in their homes, and they have no idea what's going on or how to make plans. Your clients have lives outside of the work you do! A simple misstep of a few minutes on your part can create hours of delays by the time your client is aware that things have changed.

One of the trends I noticed was HOW everyone in the field was communicating with others.

On the one hand, a client would ask specific questions about timing, and on the other, subcontractors and employees would answer vaguely. As I dug deeper, I saw email and text communications that were equally as vague.

Here's an example:

Project Manager: "When will you be done with xxx?"

Subcontractor: "I have to talk to my boss. I'll let you know."

Project Manager: "Okay."

A day passed ...

Project Manager: "Hey, any idea when you'll be done?"

Subcontractor: "By the end of the week."

Project Manager: "Okay."

Friday morning ...

Project Manager: "Are you going to be done today?"

Subcontractor: "No, we ran into a glitch. We should wrap up by Tuesday."

Project Manager: "Okay, let me know if you run into problems. The client is getting anxious."

Now, imagine for a minute, the client is paying for our project management team to be in control of the schedule ... but who's really in charge?

I'd venture to guess that seven times out of 10, it's the lowest common denominator. You got it ... it's the "helper" of the subcontractor who is either late, doesn't show up to work, or was given tasks he/she isn't capable of handling correctly.

I WAS in the field with employees who OFTEN spoke in vague promises to me. It was one of the reasons I'd fall out of integrity with my deadlines to others. My laziness for not being willing to hold others to concrete deadlines made ME ultimately responsible.

Somehow, I had to put a stop to it.

Here's how I did it (and how you can, too).

When people gave me a vague answer to a simple question, I asked them:

"When will you have it done?"

No matter their answer, I'd stay with the question and keep asking when until they gave me a DATE and a TIME.

Then, I would ask them to follow up with me if anything changed.

Often, they didn't follow up ... at least, not at first.

But when they realized I was *always* going to follow up with them, they remembered they'd made a promise, and I was going to hold them to it.

I wasn't a jerk about it, but if time had passed on their promise and I hadn't heard from them, I'd simply call or text and remind them that today, about 15 minutes ago, for example, they'd promised to be done, to deliver, etc.

During that conversation, I would RESET a time with them to have the job completed.

Sure, doing this was uncomfortable at first, but over time, I noticed something very interesting.

They began giving me dates AND times they would finish ... and more often than not, they would be good for their word.

No one likes to be the guy who feels guilty and is expecting "that" call.

The trickle-down effect ensued. The people I held accountable began communicating to their team about dates/times.

They began to implement rules to remain in integrity.

They began to UPGRADE the people on their team with those who had the same sense of integrity.

Doing the work is hard enough without also feeling like you're a dip-shit who can't make good on your word.

Maximizing YOUR time requires YOU to not allow others to waste it.

No amount of bitching, complaining, or coaching will motivate another human to value your time.

It's much simpler to NOT allow others to waste your time.

Time Management Recap

- Create deadlines with others ON EVERY task you have promised to complete for them.

- Put them in your calendar and hold yourself accountable.

- If you miss a deadline or know that you're going to, reach out to who you've made a promise to and simply reset the deadline.

- It's called INTEGRITY.

The BONUS comes in when you begin to hold others accountable as well.

You don't have to be an asshole about it either. You can simply show others the benefits THEY get for being accountable for their time management. You can show them how many fewer headaches they'll have by being extremely clear of who will do what by when.

Using this tip has helped us work at the highest levels of productivity and integrity with our clients. It's also one of the topics we discuss in our weekly meetings.

THAT's how important it is.

Chapter 25

Power Versus Force

Finding opportunity is a matter of believing it's there.
—*Barbara Corcoran*

Have you heard about the man who invented the washing machine?

No?

Well, he was called in from the fields to take care of his invalid wife and wash clothes. Then finding how laborious it was to wash by hand, he invented the washing machine and amassed a fortune for his invention.

How about the man from New Jersey who thought he could make an improvement on shears and created the electric clippers?

Michelangelo found a discarded piece of marble in Florence's streets and saw the opportunity to carve one of the most beautiful statues ever made, the figure of young David.

On the flip side, there are thousands upon thousands of stories of men and women who have decided that wealth was just around the corner. They chose to give up what they have and search for greener pastures and incredible wealth. More often than not, these people didn't find what they thought they were looking for.

You see, wherever you go, there you are! You take all your problems AND successes with you. There's nothing wrong with going to a better place with more opportunities. Just be mindful that the power lies within you, not the opportunity.

Parting Ways

Just this week, I sat down to lunch with Jim, an old business partner, to catch up and find out what he was up to and share the growth of our company. We parted ways a few years ago because we'd had different visions about growing our fledgling company. I'll be forever grateful for the time we've invested together because he helped me solidify the path we are on now.

In 2015, I founded the company Granite State Contracting and brought him on board in 2016. From 2016 until January of 2018, he and I carved out a foundation for our vision. These were rocky times with many adversities to overcome, and in January 2018, he let me know he'd started his own company, and we were parting ways. Of course, I had many emotions around it, as did he, but we both chose to keep the communication lines open and help one another out instead of becoming competitors.

As we sat there, he shared his struggles and growth that he'd experienced since 2018.

Although he's making progress, I couldn't help but detect that he has dreams and visions about a future he's not sure he will ever realize. He did tell me that his sales volume had remained steady over the last three years, while his profit had increased, so at least we had something to celebrate.

Eventually, he asked me where I was in business. I shared with him that we'd tripled our company from 2018 to 2019 and will triple again in 2020. We'd had our first-ever million-dollar sales month this year and are growing at a pace that requires me to focus on my business almost exclusively instead of in it.

That's when he broke in and said, "You're a couple of years ahead of me and doing what we planned together."

I just said, "Yeah ..."

The truth is I doubt he has ANY idea of what I've had to do to grow my business at such a rapid rate. To say that I'm a "couple of years" ahead of him suggests that given time, he'll be there, too.

It must be nice for the average person to think that they might WIN the lottery. It must be nice to believe that life is an "if-then, go-to" kind of experience or that every time you pull a lever, you get a reward. It must be nice to think that I simply followed a cookie-cutter formula to sell and service millions of dollars per business year. It must be nice for him to believe he can build it if he just bides his time and waits for the opportunity to show itself.

Here's the damn truth: opportunity is EVERYWHERE.

It's right here, right now. It isn't two years away for him, for you, or me. It's here for the man or woman who becomes FOCUSED on what they want with laser-like intent. It isn't something that you will likely trip over one day. You won't just get lucky and live happily ever after from it. It isn't found in your damn excuses, and it sure as hell isn't realized by telling yourself that you're equal to any task when you know deep down in your heart you won't pay the price for your success — that you can't commit to what needs to be done.

Too often, I believe we look for the easy path to success. We're told and sold that "we too" can have it all for $1497. We think we can exchange something we genuinely don't care about for something we do, but we fail to realize that our dream isn't bought cheaply.

Success isn't a common whore ... more like a jealous mistress!
She doesn't want half ... she requires it all:
Success requires all your focus,
all your resources, all your heart.

Once you commit to your purpose, to your burning desire... you'll get it.

Take a moment and name something that you had to have so badly it hurt, something that you eventually did whatever was required to do to have it. No matter how big or small it was, the opportunity for any goal in your life lies in a seed.

Opportunity is right here, but you might not be able to see it yet because you don't want it enough.

Remember, those who are weak wait for opportunities, those who are strong, make them.

Success is a Simple Choice

It's a beautiful reality, having those around you succeed. And it's an indicator that you're hanging out with the right people. People go through many emotions watching others grow. We're all living life, we all want to succeed, and we all want to have the results of our dreams.

I'm not getting down on anybody for having dreams, and I'm not judging anyone if they don't get the results they want.

I struggled for years trying to live my dream life. I can't tell you how many times I had an idea of what I wanted and how many times I made bad decisions or involved myself with people who were not equally passionate about my vision.

Some people had ulterior motives, and sometimes along the way, I wasn't as authentic as I needed to be either.

There are lots of reasons why I'd work hard to set myself up for success and realize some results but ultimately fail. Some of those reasons were because of me, and some were despite me. Yet, there's a precise reason why anyone ultimately gets the results they want ...

They chose not to quit.

They chose not to give up on their dream and decided instead to evolve that dream.

They chose not to listen to people who took from them. They decided not to take a momentary failure and allow it to destroy what it is they were trying to put together. The reason that I champion for people like that is that for a long time, that was me.

I've been at this entrepreneurial thing for decades now and have made a lot of mistakes. I've made choices to involve myself with people in business online and offline that have caused me a lot of pain. Many people have told me and shown me that I was doing things the wrong way. Many people have made fun of my dreams and advised that I should have done it a different way.

I bet you can say the same. There might even be people in your life right now telling you that you're doing "it" the wrong way.

It's incredible that people can give you advice about something they're not doing themselves. They have no idea what your business is. They have no idea what it is you're trying to accomplish. They have no idea how much time you spend at night thinking about what it is you're trying to do, the relationships that you're developing, and the reasons behind those relationships.

There are all sorts of intricacies they don't know about. It's because they're looking at it from 1,000 feet away that they can tell you you're doing it wrong. But what they are seeing is not relevant — because they are not experiencing what you are. I know you want to invite them to wear your shoes before they give you advice. I get it.

It's essential to listen to what everybody has to say, to take what you can and what makes sense, and leave the rest without emotionally attaching to it.

Whatever you do, don't choose to give up on your dreams.

Succeeding has very little to do with ANYONE else.

You're going to succeed because you choose to grow.

I love surrounding myself with people on the pathway to success because we're a family now. We huddle around social media via DMs, Zoom calls, text messages, and phone calls.

We purposely choose to meet in person every month, even though we live thousands of miles apart. We realize there is no price too high to push ourselves to realize the most elite version of ourselves.

We have become a family of choice, supporting and encouraging each other along our different paths. We have chosen to link arms and support each other in our quest to live a life worth having.

Even when I was going through the most challenging struggles, someone would speak to me from my family and let me know that everything was going to be okay. That's the power of being aligned with a higher purpose. That's the power of running with others who have the same core values and vision for themselves and the world we intend to change for the better.

I'm here to tell you that if you give going after what you want your best shot, there is no way you'll fail — as long as you don't quit.

Champions choose to be champions, even when they're not getting the results they want. They know they have what it takes to make it happen.

You have what it takes to make it happen. Don't EVER give up on yourself!

My hope is that you've found inspiration in this book, not motivation. I've personally found motivation to be like a good cup of coffee. It tastes great, but the energy doesn't last long.

Inspiration, on the other hand, gives YOU the keys to your own potential. You can choose to stoke that fire and keep it lit by asking more questions, taking more actions, and refining exactly what a life of significance means to you.

I'm also available to help you along that journey. Feel free to visit www.KrisWhitehead.com. On my site, you'll see opportunities to visit our private masterminds, and you can also schedule a 1:1 private call with me.

You can also read our blog and discover more insights from the front lines of running multiple businesses, living an abundant life with my family and friends, and how I'm choosing to evolve every single day.

Until we meet again, I'll see you in the trenches!

Afterword

Let's recap what I've shared with you in this book.

Pure mindset. Mindset is one of those topics that's easily talked about, but not easily followed. Most people are constantly changing their minds. They don't have goals, they have dreams, and that small change in word choice gives the average person a pressure relief valve when the going gets tough.

You've learned in this book that success is often found in HOW you choose to look at situations.

In a victim-mentality state, you're always hoping for a miracle to save you. Most of us didn't create that for ourselves. We were taught by people in authority over us, by their words, and MORE IMPORTANTLY by their actions that we can blame, shame, ridicule, and revenge our way through life.

In an ownership mentality state, you are unstoppable because you don't require anyone to blame or fix your situation. This brings the power back to YOU.

Although we didn't talk about the word ICONIC much, owning who you are and everything that happens to you shifts the focus. Instead of things happening to you, they happen FOR you. That is the beginning of living an ICONIC life. It's the beginning of being ICONIC amongst your peers and dominating your wishes into goals and goals into reality.

Being ICONIC takes you from feeling powerless and weak to knowing that you have the answers you need to make moves to secure a present and future you are content with.

Being ICONIC turns you into a leader in any situation you find yourself in because you are one of the rarest things on earth: A FREE MAN or FREE WOMAN.

Very few people are willing to do the work required to be truly free. Free of prejudices and paradigms that hold you back. Free of dogma that is set to serve those in control. Free of antiquated practices that no longer work for you or those you serve.

Becoming ICONIC is THE hard road that few take because of the discipline it requires to master. Becoming ICONIC requires you to put your ego to the side, so your innate gifts can be mastered until those talents push you to the very top of where you aim.

Welcome to the daily grind of being ICONIC.

It is going to take everything you have to give, and although the process won't always be fun, I promise it's worth it.

Always remember, no one on earth is exactly like you. No one has had your experiences, and no one else can share them exactly as you do.

Be bold enough to show the world who you are, what you stand for, and what it looks like to win on your terms.

Be bold enough to become … ICONIC.

About the Author

Kris Whitehead has tasted the bitterness of failure often enough to know it's right around any corner, on any street, ready and waiting to keep any of us down.

From dropping out of college with 13 credits to graduate to losing his first business after a decade of success, Kris learned that picking himself up after a fall is not only the best opportunity for growth; it's the BEST opportunity to show others how to rise from the ashes and become ICONIC.

He is the CEO of two multi-million-dollar companies and the Director of Coaches for Apex Executives, the fastest and most powerful Mastermind Network on the planet.

Kris attributes his success after failure to the unwavering dedication that everyone has a unique ability to influence others and bring their gifts to a world that's hungry for an "in the trenches" leadership style, teaching what YOU DO as being more important than what you say.

He's coached over 10,000 people into finding their purpose on earth and living by it no matter what. Kris has been featured in *Forbes, The Wall Street Journal*, on every major news network, and many other news publications.

Kris lives in Amherst, New Hampshire, with his wife, Robyn. They enjoy raising their three children who are in college and getting ready to impact the world in a massive way.

Disclaimer

While the author and publisher have used their best efforts in preparing this book to provide accurate information, they make no representations or warranties with respect to the accuracy or completeness of the contents.

The advice and strategies contained herein may not be suitable for your situation and are merely the opinion of the author. Consult with a professional where appropriate.

The author and publisher specifically disclaim any liability, loss, or risk, whether personal, financial or otherwise, that is incurred as a direct or indirect consequence from the use and/or application of any contents or material of this book and/or its resources.

The purchaser and/or reader of this publication assumes all responsibility and liability for the use of these materials and information.

Adherence to all applicable laws and regulations, both advertising and all other aspects of doing business in the United States or any other jurisdiction are the sole responsibility of the purchaser and/or reader.

Made in United States
Orlando, FL
11 February 2022

14729643R00095